Learn SQL (usii Le

MW01282027

SQL for Beginners with Hands-on Project
The only book you need to start coding in SQL immediately

By Jamie Chan

http://www.learncodingfast.com/sql

Preface

This book is written to help you learn SQL programming FAST and learn it WELL. We'll be using MySQL in the book, which is a free database management system that is widely used.

If you are an absolute beginner to SQL, you'll find that this book explains complex concepts in an easy to understand and concise manner. If you are an experienced coder, you'll appreciate that this book covers a wide range of topics.

Topics covered include basic concepts like table creation and data manipulation, to more advanced concepts like triggers, cursors, stored routines and more. These topics are carefully selected to give you a broad exposure to SQL, while not overwhelming you with information overload.

In addition, as Richard Branson puts it: "The best way of learning about anything is by doing". Throughout the book, we'll be building a database together. This hands-on approach to learning will help you gain a deeper understanding of the language. At the end of the course, you'll also be guided through a new project that gives you a chance to put what you've learned to use.

You can download the source code for the examples and project at
http://www.learncodingfast.com/sql

Any errata can be found at http://www.learncodingfast.com/errata

Contact Information

I would love to hear from you.
For feedback or queries, you can contact me at
jamie@learncodingfast.com.

More Books by Jamie

Python: Learn Python in One Day and Learn It Well (1st Edition)

Python: Learn Python in One Day and Learn It Well (2nd Edition)

C#: Learn C# in One Day and Learn It Well

Java: Learn Java in One Day and Learn It Well

CSS: Learn CSS in One Day and Learn It Well

Contents

Chapter 1: Introduction

Welcome to SQL and thank you so much for picking up my book. I sincerely hope that this book can help you master SQL fast and introduce you to the exciting world of databases.

This book adopts a hands-on approach to learning. As we progress from one chapter to another, we'll be doing various exercises. You are strongly encouraged to follow along these exercises.

At the end of the book, we'll also be working on a new project together. This project involves building a SQL database for a sports complex. We'll learn to build the database, insert data, perform queries, write routines, views, cursors, and more.

Excited and ready to start embarking on our SQL learning journey? Let's do it!

What is SQL?

Simply stated, SQL stands for Structured Query Language and is a language used to manage data stored in a relational database.

This brings us to the next question - What is a database?

A database is a collection of data organized in some format so that the data can be easily accessed, managed and updated. The predominant type of database is a relational database. Relational databases organize data in the form of tables. In addition, they contain queries, views and other elements to help us interact with the data.

In order to manage our database, we need to use a software application known as a database management system (DBMS).

Clear?

So far, we have the following terminologies:

1) SQL is a language
2) A database is a structured collection of data
3) A DBMS is a software that we use to manage our databases

With regards to DBMS, there are a large number of them available. Some are free to download and use while others are not. The most commonly used DBMS include MySQL, Oracle, Microsoft SQL Server and IBM DB2.

Each of these DBMS have their own versions of SQL. While this may sound intimidating, rest assured that all DBMS support the major SQL commands (such as `SELECT`, `UPDATE`, `DELETE`, `INSERT`) in a similar manner. Hence, if you know one version of SQL, it is very easy to pick up other versions.

In this book, we'll be using MySQL. This is one of the most popular DBMS available. Best of all, it's free! From this point forward, whenever I mention SQL, I'm referring to the MySQL version.

Getting Ready to Code

In order to start using MySQL, we need to first download and install two applications: MySQL Server and My SQL Workbench.

Installing MySQL applications

Windows

For Windows users, go to
https://dev.mysql.com/downloads/windows/installer/.

Scroll down and click on the first "Download" button to download the application. You'll be directed to another page. Scroll to the bottom of the page and click on "No thanks, just start my download."

Once you have downloaded the program, double-click on the file and follow the instructions to install the software.

When prompted to choose a setup type, select "Custom" and click "Next".

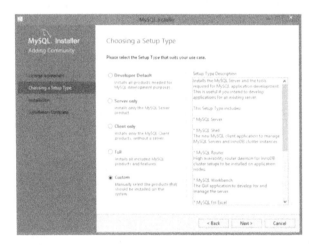

You'll be asked to select the products and features to install.

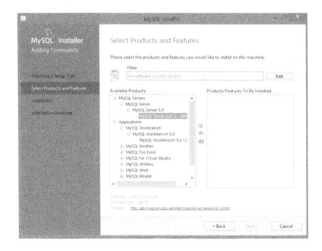

Under "Available Products", fully expand "MySQL Servers" by clicking on the + signs. Once fully expanded, click on the last item and click on the green arrow to move this item to the "Products/Features To Be Installed" section.

Next, expand "Applications" and fully expand "MySQL Workbench". Click on the last item and click on the green arrow to move this item to the "Products/Features To Be Installed" section.

Once you are done, click on "Next" and follow the instructions to continue with the installation. Stick to the default options selected at each stage.

When prompted to enter a password, enter your desired password and jot down the password. You'll need this password later.

Click on "Next" to continue and complete the installation.

Mac OS

For Mac users, to install MySQL Server, go to https://dev.mysql.com/downloads/mysql/.

Scroll down and click on the first "Download" button to download the application.

Once you do that, you'll be directed to another page. Scroll to the bottom of the page and click on "No thanks, just start my download."

Once you have downloaded the program, double-click on the file to unzip it. Next, double-click on the unzipped file and follow the instructions to install the software. At the configuration stage, choose "Use Strong Password Encryption" and click "Next". Enter your desired password and jot down the password. You'll need this password later. Ensure that the "Start MySQL Server once the installation is complete" option is selected and click on "Finish" to complete the installation.

Once you are done installing MySQL Server, you need to install another software known as MySQL Workbench. This software provides us with a graphical user interface to make it easier for us to interact with MySQL. To download MySQL Workbench, go to https://dev.mysql.com/downloads/workbench/.

Click on the first "Download" button to download the application. Once again, you'll be directed to another page. Scroll to the bottom of the page and click on "No thanks, just start my download." to download the program. Double-click on the downloaded file and follow the instructions to install it after downloading.

Launching MySQL Workbench

Once you have installed the necessary applications, we are ready to do some coding.

First, launch MySQL Workbench.

You'll get the screen below:

Click on the grey rectangle under "MySQL Connections" (named "Local instance 3306" in the image above). You'll be prompted for a password. Enter the password that you keyed in previously when you installed MySQL Server and select "Save password in vault" (or "Save password in keychain" for Mac users). Next, press OK to proceed. If all goes well, you should be directed to the screen below:

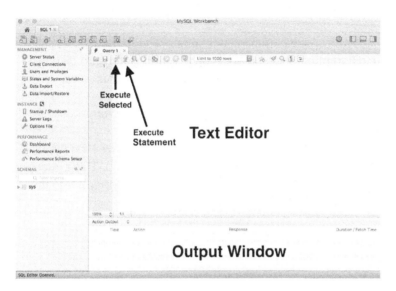

The main area is a text editor where we'll be entering our SQL commands. The window below is the output window (refer to screenshot above).

Got that?

Great!

Writing our first MySQL code

Now, we are ready to get our feet wet and write some SQL code.

Type the following lines into the text editor (for the first line, be sure to add a space after the two hyphens):

```
-- Using SELECT to display messages
SELECT 'Hello World';
SELECT 'MySQL is fun!';
```

You should notice that the first line is in gray while the word SELECT is in blue and 'Hello World' and 'MySQL is fun!' are in green.

This is the software's way of making our code easier to read. Different words serve different purposes in our program, hence they are displayed using different colors. We'll go into more details in later chapters.

There are two ways to run the SQL commands that we wrote.

The first is to select all the code that we want to run and click on the "Execute Selected" button (the button with a lightning bolt). This button should normally be located to the right of the "Save" button (refer to the previous screenshot).

This will execute all the code that is selected. You'll see a new panel called "Result Grid", with two tabs as shown below:

These two tabs give the results of the last two lines of code that we wrote (i.e. the two lines that start with the word SELECT).

The first line of code that we wrote does not give any result as it is a comment. We'll talk about comments in the next section.

Besides running all the code at one go, you can also choose to execute them one by one. To do that, simply position your cursor on the line that you want to execute and click on the "Execute Statement" button to run that statement. The "Execute Statement" button shows a lightning bolt and a cursor and is located to the right of the "Execute Selected" button.

For instance, if you place your cursor as shown in the image below

```
-- Using SELECT to display messages
SELECT 'Hello World';
SELECT 'MySQL is fun!';
```

and click on the "Execute Statement" button, you'll get a single tab in the "Result Grid" that displays the message `Hello World`.

Comments

Now that we know how to execute SQL statements, we are ready to start learning some SQL commands. However, before we do that, there's more one concept that I'll like to cover - comments.

As mentioned previously, the first line in the code that we wrote (`-- Using SELECT to display messages`) is a comment.

Comments are written to make our code more readable for other programmers. They are meant for humans only and are ignored by the DBMS.

To add comments to our program, we type two hyphens, followed by a space, as demonstrated in the example above.

Alternatively, we can also use the # symbol as shown below:

```
# This is another way to add comment
```

Last, but not least, if we want to type multiple lines comments, we can use the /*...*/ symbols:

```
/* This is a comment
This is also a comment
This is the third comment */
```

Chapter 2: Defining the Database

Now that we have a basic understand of MySQL, let's start learning some SQL commands.

How to Use this Book

Throughout this book, we'll be building a database called *companyHR* that has two tables - **employees** and **mentorships**.

The database will be used to demonstrate most of the concepts covered. Hence, you are strongly encouraged to follow along and try out the various examples.

To do that, first create a folder on your desktop and name it *MySQLExamples*.

Next, launch *MySQL Workbench* and create a new file by clicking on *File > New Query Tab* and save this file as *practice.sql* (*File > Save Script As...*) in the *MySQLExamples* folder.

*** Examples that you should try will be **presented in bold**. Whenever you see code presented in bold, you should type them into *practice.sql* and execute them yourself to try them out (even when not prompted to do so). ***

The source file for all code presented in bold can be downloaded from http://www.learncodingfast.com/sql.

Code that is not in bold is purely for demonstration purposes. You should not try them as they may alter the structure or content of our database.

Clear? Let's do it!

Creating the Database

The first thing that we need to learn is to create a database.

A database is a collection of related tables, queries and views etc.

You can think of it as being similar to an Excel workbook. An Excel workbook contains related worksheets and charts while a database contains related tables, queries and other objects (such as views and stored routines).

To create a database in MySQL, we use the `CREATE DATABASE` keywords. A keyword is a word that has a predefined meaning in SQL. In other words, if you want to create a database, you have to type `CREATE DATABASE`, you cannot be creative and type other words like `MAKE DATABASE` or `CREATE COLLECTION` etc.

Keywords are generally not case sensitive in SQL. Hence, you can also write `create database` or `CREATE database`. However, the common practice is to use uppercase for keywords. That's the convention that we'll be following in this book. For all the syntaxes presented in this book, any word that is in uppercase is a keyword.

The syntax to create a database is shown below:

```
CREATE DATABASE name_of_database;
```

For instance, to create a database called *companyHR*, we write:

CREATE DATABASE companyHR;

This is known as a SQL statement. SQL statements always end with a semi-colon (;) unless otherwise stated.

Type this statement into *practice.sql* and execute it. You should get

```
CREATE DATABASE companyHR      1 row(s) affected
```

in the output window with a green tick on the left. The green tick indicates that the statement is executed correctly.

Using the Database

After we create a database, we have to let the DBMS know that we want to use this database. This is because the DBMS may be managing more than one databases concurrently. We have to let it know that all subsequent code that we write applies to the stated database.

To do that, we use the following syntax:

```
USE name_of_database;
```

For instance, to use the *companyHR* database, we write

```
USE companyHR;
```

Deleting the Database

Now, suppose after you create your database, you realise that you have typed the name wrongly. There is no easy way to rename a database in MySQL. What you can do is create a new database and delete the old database. To delete a database, we use the syntax

```
DROP DATABASE [IF EXISTS] name_of_database;
```

You can see that we used square brackets [ ] in the DROP DATABASE syntax above. These brackets will be used throughout the book to indicate optional content.

In other words, when deleting a database, the IF EXISTS keywords are optional. We use them to prevent an error from occurring when we accidentally try to delete a database that does not exist.

For instance, to delete a database called *wrongDB*, we write

```
DROP DATABASE IF EXISTS wrongDB;
```

However, if we are certain that *wrongDB* exists, we can simply write

```
DROP DATABASE wrongDB;
```

Chapter 3: Defining Tables

In the previous chapter, we learned to create and use a database. In this chapter, we'll learn to add tables to our database. We'll also learn to alter and delete the tables if necessary. This is a relatively long chapter, so take your time to slowly go through it.

Creating Tables

First, let's look at how we can create tables to add to our database. To create a table, we use the following syntax:

```
CREATE TABLE table_name (
    column_name1 datatype [column constraints],
    column_name2 datatype [column constraints],
    ...
    [table constraints],
    [table constraints]
);
```

Let's discuss the syntax in detail.

Tables in SQL databases are organized in rows and columns. Suppose we want to create a table to store information about the employees of a company. We can design the table as shown below:

id	em_name	gender	contact_number	age	date_created
1	James Lee	M	516-514-6568	23	2007-09-21 11:20:46
2	Peter Pasternak	M	845-644-7919	21	2008-09-12 22:23:20
3	Clara Couto	F	845-641-5236	36	2010-11-01 16:13:45
4	Walker Welch	M		42	2014-10-30 13:41:23
5	Li Xiao Ting	F	646-218-7733	20	2014-11-30 14:40:23

Each column in the table stores a specific piece of information about the employee (such as the id, name and gender of the employee).

Each row, on the other hand, stores information about one employee. A row is sometimes also referred to as a record.

Specifying Columns

When we create the table, we need to specify the columns. For each column, we need to state the data type and any constraints that the column must satisfy.

Data Types

Let's first look at data types.

Data type refers to the type of data that the column stores. For instance, the first column in the previous table (`id`) stores numerical information. The second column (`em_name`) stores textual information.

In MySQL, there are a number of commonly used data types:

Textual data types

Textual information, also known as strings, are commonly stored using the `CHAR` or `VARCHAR` data type in MySQL. They can contain letters, numbers or special characters.

`CHAR(size)`

`CHAR` stands for "character" and is used to store a fixed length string of up to 255 characters. The desired length is specified in parentheses after the `CHAR` keyword.

If you try to store a string that is longer than the specified length, you'll get an error.

If you store a string that is shorter than the specified length, the string will be right-padded with spaces.

For instance, if you specify a column as `CHAR(5)` but use it to store a string like `'NY'`, it will be stored as `'NY   '`. However, when the string is subsequently retrieved, these spaces will not be displayed.

VARCHAR(size)

`VARCHAR` is another data type for storing strings. It holds a <u>variable length</u> string and can store up to 255 characters. You have to specify the maximum length in parentheses.

In contrast to `CHAR(5)`, if you specify a column as `VARCHAR(5)` and use it to store the string `'NY'`, it will be stored as `'NY'` with no spaces added.

As you can see, `VARCHAR` is more flexible and uses less storage than `CHAR` in most cases. However, it can be slower than `CHAR`.

In most cases, if you are storing strings that are of fixed lengths (e.g. gender represented as `'M'` or `'F'` or state abbreviations such as `'NY'`, `'AL'`, `'AK'` etc), you should use `CHAR`. Otherwise, you should use `VARCHAR`.

<u>Numerical data types</u>

Next, let's look at numbers. Numbers in MySQL are commonly stored using `INT`, `FLOAT`, `DOUBLE` or `DECIMAL`.

INT

`INT` stands for integers (i.e. numbers with no fractional parts) and can hold numbers from `-2147483648` to `2147483647`.

If we specify a column as `INT UNSIGNED`, it can hold values from `0` to `4294967295`.

FLOAT(m, d)

FLOAT is used to store non integers (i.e. numbers with fractional parts). It uses 4 bytes of storage.

In MySQL, you can specify two parameters - m and d - when defining FLOAT.

m refers to the total number of digits the FLOAT stores while d refers to the number of digits after the decimal point.

For instance, if you store a number – say 12.34567 – as FLOAT(5, 3), it will be rounded off to 12.346 (i.e. 5 digits in total, three of which are after the decimal point).

FLOAT stores numbers as approximate values. It is accurate up to about 7 decimal places.

Hence, if you use FLOAT(10, 9) to store 1.23456789999, it may be stored as 1.234567881.

This discrepancy is not due to rounding (as 1.23456789999 when rounded off to 9 decimal places should be 1.234567900). Instead, this discrepancy is due to the fact that floats are stored as approximate values.

DOUBLE(m, d)

DOUBLE is also used to store non integers as approximate values. It uses 8 bytes of storage and can be used to store numbers with higher precision. It is accurate up to about 14 decimal places. Similar to FLOAT, you can specify the total number of digits (m) and the number of digits after the decimal point (d).

DECIMAL(m, d)

DECIMAL is used to store non-integers as <u>exact values</u>. Similar to FLOAT and DOUBLE, you can specify the total number of digits (m) and the number of digits after the decimal point (d) when using DECIMAL.

DECIMAL is commonly used to store monetary data where precision is important.

Date and Time data types

Next, let's look at date and time data types.

YEAR

The YEAR data type is used to store a year in either a two-digit or a four-digit format. Values allowed in four-digit format are from 1901 to 2155. Values allowed in two-digit format are from 1 to 69 (representing years from 2001 to 2069) and 70 to 99 (representing years from 1970 to 1999).

DATE

The DATE datatype is used to store a date in the YYYY-MM-DD format, with a supported range of '1000-01-01' to '9999-12-31'.

TIME

The TIME data type is used to store time in the HH:MI:SS format, with a supported range of '-838:59:59' to '838:59:59'.

DATETIME

The DATETIME data type is used to store a date and time combination in the YYYY-MM-DD HH:MI:SS format. The supported range is from '1000-01-01 00:00:00' to '9999-12-31 23:59:59'.

`TIMESTAMP`

The `TIMESTAMP` data type is also used to store a date and time combination in the `YYYY-MM-DD HH:MI:SS` format. The supported range is from `'1970-01-01 00:00:01'` UTC to `'2038-01-09 03:14:07'` UTC.

One of the main differences between `DATETIME` and `TIMESTAMP` is that MySQL converts `TIMESTAMP` values from the current time zone to UTC for storage, and back from UTC to the current time zone for retrieval. It does not do so for `DATETIME` values.

Hence, for instance, if a user is in the UTC+4 time zone and stores a `TIMESTAMP` as `'2018-04-11 09:00:00'`, someone in the UTC time zone will see this data as `'2018-04-11 05:00:00'`.

In contrast, if the data is stored using the `DATETIME` data type, all users will see the data as `'2018-04-11 09:00:00'` regardless of which time zone they are in.

This unique conversion feature of the `TIMESTAMP` data type makes it very useful for databases that are used by users across different time zones. It is also commonly used to record information about when a piece of data was inserted into the database.

Column Constraints

Now that we understand data types, let's move on to column constraints.

Besides specifying the data type of each column, we can also add constraints for those columns. These constraints are requirements that the columns must satisfy. Each constraint must be specified using predefined keywords in MySQL.

Some of the constraints include:

NOT NULL

Specifies that a column cannot be empty. In other words, it must have a value for all rows.

UNIQUE

Specifies that all values in the column must be unique.

DEFAULT

Sets a default value for a column when no value is specified.

PRIMARY KEY

Specifies that the column is a primary key. A primary key <u>uniquely identifies each row</u> in a table.

For instance, if we are designing a database for a company and we have a table that stores information about each employee, we can use employee ID as a primary key, assuming that each employee has a different ID.

However, we cannot use employee name as the primary key as it is possible for two employees to have the same name.

A primary key is by default NOT NULL and UNIQUE; there is no need to explicitly state these two constraints if the column is a primary key. In addition, each table can only have one primary key.

AUTO_INCREMENT

Specifies that the values for this column should be automatically increased by 1 for each new record. This feature is often used to generate a primary key for the table. By default, the starting value for an auto increment column is 1. We'll learn how to change this starting value in the next chapter.

Each table can only have one auto increment column and that column must be defined as a key (such as a primary key or a unique key).

Now that we know how to specify the columns of a table, let us create our first table - **co_employees**.

Note that we'll temporarily name this table **co_employees** instead of **employees** as mentioned in Chapter 2. This is because we'll learn to change the table name later.

For now, the **co_employees** table has the following columns:

```
id: INT
em_name: VARCHAR(255)
gender: CHAR(1)
contact_number: VARCHAR(255)
age: INT
date_created: TIMESTAMP
```

All columns of the table cannot be null except for the `contact_number` column.

In addition, the `id` column is a primary key and is auto incremented.

Finally, the `date_created` column has a default value provided by the `NOW()` function.

A function is a block of code that performs a certain task. The `NOW()` function is a built-in function that comes with MySQL (i.e. it is already pre-coded for us). It gives us the current date and time whenever it is being used (i.e. whenever a new record is inserted into the table). We'll talk more about built-in functions in Chapter 6. For now, let's just use the function in our table creation code.

To create the table, we use the code below:

```
CREATE TABLE co_employees (
    id INT PRIMARY KEY AUTO_INCREMENT,
```

```
    em_name VARCHAR(255) NOT NULL,
    gender CHAR(1) NOT NULL,
    contact_number VARCHAR(255),
    age INT NOT NULL,
    date_created TIMESTAMP NOT NULL DEFAULT NOW()
);
```

Copy the code into *practice.sql* and execute it to create the
co_employees table yourself.

To execute this statement, simply place your cursor anywhere within the
statement and click on the 'Execute Statement' button (refer to Chapter 1
if you have forgotten where the 'Execute Statement' button is).

Specifying Table Constraints

Next, let's move on to learn more complex concepts in table creation.

In the previous section, we learned that when we create a table, we need
to specify the data types of the columns. In addition, we can also add
column constraints like NOT NULL and PRIMARY KEY to our columns.

Beside column constraints, we can also specify table constraints when
creating a table. Table constraints are similar to column constraints
except that they can affect more than one column.

Let's look at some of the common table constraints in MySQL.

Primary Key Constraint

The first table constraint is the primary key constraint.

Previously when discussing column constraints, we learned that if a
particular column is a primary key, we add the words PRIMARY KEY
when we create the column. However, there is another way to do it. This
second method is useful if the primary key is made up of two or more
columns.

Suppose we have a table that stores information about the mentor-mentee relationships of employees in a company. We may have a table as shown below:

mentor_id	mentee_id	status	project
1	2	Ongoing	SQF Limited
1	3	Past	Wayne Fibre
2	3	Ongoing	SQF Limited
3	4	Ongoing	SQF Limited
6	5	Past	Flynn Tech

Let's call this table **mentorships**.

If you study the **mentorships** table, you will notice that no column is suitable to be used as a primary key. This is because a primary key has to uniquely identify each row; no row satisfies this requirement.

For instance, we cannot use `mentor_id` as the primary key as two different rows (rows 1 and 2) have the same `mentor_id`. The same applies to the `mentee_id`, `status` and `project` columns.

What can we do in this case?

What we can do is use the combination of 2 or more columns as the primary key, as long as we can be certain that no two rows will have the same values for this combination of columns.

For instance, we can use the combination of the `mentor_id`, `mentee_id` and `project` as the primary key.

When we do that, we will not be allowed to input two rows with the same `mentor_id`, `mentee_id`, `project` combination. For instance, if we add another row with the values

```
mentor_id = 1
mentee_id = 2
project = 'SQF Limited'
```

we'll get an error as the first row in the table already has this combination.

In order to state that the three columns (`mentor_id`, `mentee_id`, `project`) together form the primary key, we can add the following table constraint when creating the table:

```
PRIMARY KEY(mentor_id, mentee_id, project)
```

This is another way of specifying the primary key of a table and is most useful when the primary key is made up of multiple columns.

Foreign Key Constraint

Next, let's look at how we can add foreign key constraints to our **mentorships** table.

First, what is a foreign key?

In the **mentorships** table, we can see that `mentor_id` 1 is a mentor to two mentees (`mentee_id` 2 and 3). However, this information is not very useful as we have no idea who 1, 2 and 3 are.

Now, suppose we know that the **mentorships** table is related to the **co_employees** table and that `mentor_id` and `mentee_id` are both taken from the `id` column of the **co_employees** table.

We can then refer to the **co_employees** table and see that employees 1, 2 and 3 are `James Lee`, `Peter Pasternak` and `Clara Couto` respectively. From the **mentorships** table, we know that `James Lee` is a mentor to `Peter Pasternak` and `Clara Couto`.

How can we describe this relationship between the two tables in MySQL?

We use foreign keys.

A foreign key is a column (or a collection of columns) in one table that links to the primary key in another table.

In our example, `mentor_id` and `mentee_id` in the **mentorships** table are foreign keys as their values are actually taken from the primary key (`id`) in the **co_employees** table.

To specify that `mentor_id` and `mentee_id` are foreign keys, we add the code below when creating the **mentorships** table:

```
FOREIGN KEY(mentor_id) REFERENCES co_employees(id) ON
DELETE CASCADE ON UPDATE RESTRICT,
FOREIGN KEY(mentee_id) REFERENCES co_employees(id) ON
DELETE CASCADE ON UPDATE RESTRICT
```

These two lines specify that `mentor_id` and `mentee_id` are foreign keys and that they reference the `id` column in the **co_employees** table.

When done this way, the **co_employees** table is known as the parent table and the **mentorships** table is known as the child table.

Stating that `mentor_id` and `mentee_id` are foreign keys add a restriction to them. We will not be allowed to add a record to the **mentorships** table if the `mentor_id` or `mentee_id` does not exist in the **co_employees** table.

For instance, if the **co_employees** table does not have a row with `id = 16`, we can't add the following record

```
mentor_id = 1
mentee_id = 16
status = 'Ongoing'
project = 'SQF Limited'
```

to our **mentorships** table as this mentee has a `mentee_id` of `16`.

Next, note that we also added the `ON DELETE CASCADE` and `ON UPDATE RESTRICT` clauses to our foreign keys.

The ON DELETE CASCADE clause means that if a certain employee is deleted from the **co_employees** table (the parent table), any record of that employee in the **mentorships** table will also be deleted. Hence, if we delete employee 3 in the **co_employees** table, the second, third and fourth rows in the **mentorships** table will also be deleted.

Besides the ON DELETE CASCADE clause, there are other ON DELETE clauses that we can add to a foreign key. These clauses include:

ON DELETE RESTRICT - The row in the parent table cannot be deleted if a row in the child table references that parent row.

ON DELETE SET NULL - The child row foreign key value will be set to NULL if the parent row is deleted. For this to work, the relevant column in the child row must allow for NULL values.

ON DELETE SET DEFAULT - The child row foreign key value will be set to the default value if the parent row is deleted.

These ON DELETE clauses can also be applied when updating the parent table. To do that, we use the ON UPDATE clause.

For instance, in our example, we added the ON UPDATE RESTRICT clause to our foreign keys. This means that we will not be allowed to update the primary key in the parent table if there is at least one row in the child table that references it.

We'll try some of these examples when we insert, update and delete data from our **co_employees** and **mentorships** tables in the next chapter.

Unique Constraint

Next, let's talk about the unique constraint.

Suppose for the **mentorships** table, we do not want the same mentor to mentor a mentee more than once. For instance, we do not want the following case:

```
mentor_id = 1
mentee_id = 2
project = 'SQF Limited'

mentor_id = 1
mentee_id = 2
project = 'Flynn Tech'
```

We can use a UNIQUE constraint and require that the combination of mentor_id and mentee_id be unique.

To do that, we need to add the following constraint to our CREATE TABLE statement when creating the **mentorships** table:

```
UNIQUE (mentor_id, mentee_id)
```

This will ensure that we cannot have more than one row with the same mentor_id, mentee_id combination.

Some readers may notice that a UNIQUE constraint is very similar to a PRIMARY KEY constraint. Indeed, a primary key is unique by definition.

However, one of the main differences between a primary key and a unique key is that a table can only have one primary key but can have multiple unique keys.

Named Constraints

Finally, let's look at named constraints.

In the previous examples, we added table constraints without naming them. If we want, we can name our constraints. To do that, we add the following syntax before stating the constraint:

```
CONSTRAINT name_of_constraint
```

For the `UNIQUE` constraint in the previous example, we could have named it `mm_constraint` as shown below:

```
CONSTRAINT mm_constraint UNIQUE (mentor_id,
mentee_id)
```

For the `FOREIGN KEY` constraint, we could have named it `fk1`:

```
CONSTRAINT fk1 FOREIGN KEY(mentor_id) REFERENCES
co_employees(id) ON DELETE CASCADE ON UPDATE RESTRICT
```

This will make it easier to refer to the constraint in future (such as when we want to update or delete the constraint).

We'll now create the **mentorships** table.

This table has the following columns:

```
mentor_id: INT
mentee_id: INT
status: VARCHAR(255)
project: VARCHAR(255)
```

All columns cannot be null.

The primary key of the table is made up of three columns: `mentor_id`, `mentee_id` and `project`.

`mentor_id` and `mentee_id` are both foreign keys that reference the `id` column in the **co_employees** table.

In addition, we do not allow a parent row to be updated if there's a child row that references it. We also want the child row to be deleted if the parent row is deleted.

Next, we do not want the same mentor to mentor a mentee more than once.

Last but not least, we want the foreign keys and unique constraint to be named.

The code to create the table is:

```
CREATE TABLE mentorships (
    mentor_id INT NOT NULL,
    mentee_id INT NOT NULL,
    status VARCHAR(255) NOT NULL,
    project VARCHAR(255) NOT NULL,

    PRIMARY KEY (mentor_id, mentee_id, project),
    CONSTRAINT fk1 FOREIGN KEY(mentor_id) REFERENCES
co_employees(id) ON DELETE CASCADE ON UPDATE
RESTRICT,
    CONSTRAINT fk2 FOREIGN KEY(mentee_id) REFERENCES
co_employees(id) ON DELETE CASCADE ON UPDATE
RESTRICT,
    CONSTRAINT mm_constraint UNIQUE(mentor_id,
mentee_id)
);
```

Altering Tables

We've covered quite a bit in this chapter so far. To recap, we learned that to create a table, we need to do two things:

1) Specify the columns by stating their names, data types and constraints (if any)
2) Specify any table constraints that the table must fulfil

Now that we have created the two tables that we need, let's move on to learn how we can modify tables. This is useful if we need to make any changes to our tables after creating them.

Table Names

The first thing we can modify is the table name. To do that, we use the syntax

```
RENAME TABLE old_name TO new_name;
```

Let's change the name of our **co_employees** table to **employees** now. To do that, execute the following statement:

RENAME TABLE co_employees TO employees;

Columns and Table Constraints

Next, let's learn to alter some of the columns and table constraints of our tables. For each of the alterations below, we need to first write

```
ALTER TABLE table_name
```

followed by

`AUTO_INCREMENT = starting_value` to change the starting value of the auto increment column,

`ADD CONSTRAINT [name of constraint] details_of_constraint` to add a table constraint (including foreign key constraints),

`DROP INDEX name_of_constraint` to drop a table constraint (excluding foreign key constraints),

`DROP FOREIGN KEY name_of_foreign_key` to drop a foreign key constraint,

MODIFY COLUMN column_name data_type [constraints] to modify a column,

DROP COLUMN column_name to drop a column, and

ADD COLUMN column_name data_type [constraints] to add a column.

When adding a column, we can specify the position of the new column by adding the keyword FIRST after the column constraints to indicate that the new column should be the first column.

Alternatively, we can also add the AFTER column_name keywords to insert the new column after another column.

Let's look at some examples now. We'll modify the **employees** table first. Suppose we want to do the following:

1) Drop the age column
2) Add another column called salary which is of FLOAT type and cannot be null. This column should come after the contact_number column
3) Add a new column called years_in_company which is of INT type and cannot be null. This column should come after the salary column

Here's how we do it:

```
ALTER TABLE employees
    DROP COLUMN age,
    ADD COLUMN salary FLOAT NOT NULL AFTER
contact_number,
    ADD COLUMN years_in_company INT NOT NULL AFTER
salary;
```

After modifying our table, we can check if our modifications are correct by asking MySQL to describe our table.

The syntax is simply

```
DESCRIBE table_name;
```

To describe the **employees** table, we write

```
DESCRIBE employees;
```

We should get the following:

Field	Type	Null	Key	Default	Extra
id	int(11)	NO	PRI	NULL	auto_increment
em_name	varchar(255)	NO		NULL	
gender	char(1)	NO		NULL	
contact_nu...	varchar(255)	YES		NULL	
salary	float	NO		NULL	
years_in_co...	int(11)	NO		NULL	
date_created	timestamp	NO		CURRENT_TIMESTAMP	

Next, let's alter the **mentorships** table. For this table, we want to

1) Modify `fk2` by changing `ON UPDATE RESTRICT` to `ON UPDATE CASCADE`
2) Drop the `mm_constraint` constraint

In order to modify the foreign key constraint, we have to first drop the original foreign key using the statement below:

```
ALTER TABLE mentorships
   DROP FOREIGN KEY fk2;
```

Next, using a new `ALTER` statement (we are not allowed to drop and add a foreign key with the same name using a single `ALTER` statement), we add the foreign key back with the modified conditions. In addition, we also drop the `mm_constraint` constraint:

```
ALTER TABLE mentorships
   ADD CONSTRAINT fk2 FOREIGN KEY(mentee_id)
REFERENCES employees(id) ON DELETE CASCADE ON UPDATE
CASCADE,
   DROP INDEX mm_constraint;
```

Add the two ALTER statements above to *practice.sql* and execute them one by one to alter the **mentorships** table as required.

Deleting Tables

Last but not least, before we end this chapter, let's learn to delete a table. To do that, we use the syntax below:

```
DROP TABLE [IF EXISTS] table_name;
```

For instance, if we want to delete a table called **demo**, we write

```
DROP TABLE IF EXISTS demo;
```

With this, we've come to the end of Chapter 3.

Chapter 4: Inserting, Updating and Deleting Data

In the previous two chapters, we learned to create, alter and drop our databases and tables. In this chapter, we'll learn to insert data into our tables. We'll also learn to update and delete data.

Inserting Data

To insert data into MySQL, we use the following syntax:

```
INSERT INTO table_name (column1, column2, column3, …)
VALUES (value1, value2, value3, …);
```

id	em_name	gender	contact_number	salary	years_in_ company	date_created
1	James Lee	M	516-514-6568	3500	11	2007-09-21 11:20:46
2	Peter Pasternak	M	845-644-7919	6010	10	2008-09-12 22:23:20
3	Clara Couto	F	845-641-5236	3900	8	2010-11-01 16:13:45
4	Walker Welch	M		2500	4	2014-10-30 13:41:23
5	Li Xiao Ting	F	646-218-7733	5600	4	2014-11-30 14:40:23
6	Joyce Jones	F	523-172-2191	8000	3	2015-06-22 12:21:46
7	Jason Cerrone	M	725-441-7172	7980	2	2016-01-25 15:22:16
8	Prudence Phelps	F	546-312-5112	11000	2	2016-09-12 12:20:22
9	Larry Zucker	M	817-267-9799	3500	1	2017-03-12 11:18:16
10	Serena Parker	F	621-211-7342	12000	1	2017-10-18 18:14:23

Suppose we want to insert the information above into the **employees** table, we write

```
INSERT INTO employees (em_name, gender,
contact_number, salary, years_in_company) VALUES
('James Lee', 'M', '516-514-6568', 3500, 11),
('Peter Pasternak', 'M', '845-644-7919', 6010, 10),
('Clara Couto', 'F', '845-641-5236', 3900, 8),
('Walker Welch', 'M', NULL, 2500, 4),
```

```
('Li Xiao Ting', 'F', '646-218-7733', 5600, 4),
('Joyce Jones', 'F', '523-172-2191', 8000, 3),
('Jason Cerrone', 'M', '725-441-7172', 7980, 2),
('Prudence Phelps', 'F', '546-312-5112', 11000, 2),
('Larry Zucker', 'M', '817-267-9799', 3500, 1),
('Serena Parker', 'F', '621-211-7342', 12000, 1);
```

Type the statement above into *practice.sql* and execute it to insert these information into your **employees** table.

In the code above,

`table_name` is replaced by **employees**
`column1, column2, column3, ...` is replaced by **em_name, gender, contact_number, salary, years_in_company**
`value1, value2, value3, ...` is replaced by **'James Lee'**, **'M'**, **'516-514-6568'**, **3500, 11** etc

Study the code carefully.

Notice that we did not input values for `id` and `date_created`. This is because `id` is automatically generated by the system (`AUTO_INCREMENT`) while `date_created` has a `DEFAULT` value provided by the `NOW()` function.

In addition, note that we need to use quotation marks for textual information (e.g. `'James Lee'`, `'M'`, `'516-514-6568'` etc) but not for numerical information (e.g. `11`).

Finally, we inserted a record with a missing contact number (`'Walker Welch'`, `'M'`, `NULL`, `2500`, `4`) using the `NULL` keyword. This is allowed because the `contact_number` column does not have the `NOT NULL` constraint.

Next, let's try inserting data into the **mentorships** table. Suppose we want to insert the following data into the **mentorships** table, how can we do it?

mentor_id	mentee_id	status	project
1	2	Ongoing	SQF Limited
1	3	Past	Wayne Fibre
2	3	Ongoing	SQF Limited
3	4	Ongoing	SQF Limited
6	5	Past	Flynn Tech

Based on what we've learned so far, we can do it as follows:

```
INSERT INTO mentorships (mentor_id, mentee_id,
status, project) VALUES
(1, 2, 'Ongoing', 'SQF Limited'),
(1, 3, 'Past', 'Wayne Fibre'),
(2, 3, 'Ongoing', 'SQF Limited'),
(3, 4, 'Ongoing', 'SQF Limited'),
(6, 5, 'Past', 'Flynn Tech');
```

However, there is a shorter way to do it. We can omit the column names as shown below:

```
INSERT INTO mentorships VALUES
(1, 2, 'Ongoing', 'SQF Limited'),
(1, 3, 'Past', 'Wayne Fibre'),
(2, 3, 'Ongoing', 'SQF Limited'),
(3, 4, 'Ongoing', 'SQF Limited'),
(6, 5, 'Past', 'Flynn Tech');
```

This second method works only if we are inserting data for all columns. In addition, the values must be in the correct order. Else, the data will be assigned to the wrong column.

For instance, if we insert the first row as

```
(1, 2, 'SQF Limited', 'Ongoing')
```

MySQL is going to assign 'SQF Limited' to the status column and 'Ongoing' to the project column, which is not what we want.

Type either (but not both) of the INSERT statement above into *practice.sql* and execute it. That'll insert the necessary data into the **mentorships** table.

Updating Data

Next, let's look at how we can update our data. To do that, we use the syntax below:

```
UPDATE table_name
SET column1 = value1, column2 = value2, …
WHERE condition;
```

For instance, suppose we want to update the contact number of 'James Lee' from '516-514-6568' to '516-514-1729', we use the code

UPDATE employees
SET contact_number = '516-514-1729'
WHERE id = 1;

Here, we use the id column to identify 'James Lee'. We can also use other columns. For instance, we can write

```
WHERE years_in_company = 11
```

since there is only one employee with that number of years in the company.

However, if there is more than one employee with the same number of years, we'll end up updating the contact numbers of all such employees, which is not what we want.

In addition, if we omit the WHERE clause, we'll end up updating the contact numbers of ALL employees, which is also not what we want.

Deleting Data

Finally, let's look at how we can delete data from a table. To do that, we use the syntax below:

```
DELETE FROM table_name
WHERE condition;
```

For instance, to delete `'Li Xiao Ting'` (id = 5) from the **employees** table, we use the following code:

```
DELETE FROM employees
WHERE id = 5;
```

Try it yourself. You should get a green tick with the message

```
1 row(s) affected
```

in your output window.

Constraints

Now that we know how to insert, update and delete data from our tables, let's revisit some of the constraints that we placed on our tables when we created them.

Remember that we have two foreign key constraints for the **mentorships** table? Let's see how they work.

Try inserting the following data into **mentorships**:

```
INSERT INTO mentorships VALUES
(4, 21, 'Ongoing', 'Flynn Tech');
```

What happens? You get an error message that says

```
Error Code: 1452. Cannot add or update a child row: a
foreign key constraint fails
```

right? This is due to the fact that we do not have an employee with `id = 21` in the **employees** table. Hence, we cannot insert a row with `mentee_id = 21` into the **mentorships** table as the `mentee_id` column is supposed to reference the `id` column in the **employees** table.

Next, let's try to update some data in the **employees** table. For instance, try adding the code below to *practice.sql* and execute it.

```
UPDATE employees
SET id = 12
WHERE id = 1;
```

It fails too right?

This is due to the ON UPDATE RESTRICT clause that we added to the first foreign key (`fk1`) in the **mentorships** table. This foreign key links the `mentor_id` column in the **mentorships** table with the `id` column in the **employees** table.

We are not allowed to update the `id` column in the **employees** table for `id = 1` as we have two rows in the **mentorships** table that reference it (the first and second rows, with `mentor_id = 1`).

Clear? Good!

Let's move on to the ON UPDATE CASCADE clause that we added to the second foreign key (`fk2`).

Try executing the statement below:

```
UPDATE employees
SET id = 11
WHERE id = 4;
```

Here, we try to update the `id` column in the **employees** table for `id = 4`.

This update works because employee 4 is not a mentor in the **mentorships** table. Hence, it is <u>not affected</u> by the first foreign key.

However, as employee 4 is a mentee in the **mentorships** table, it is affected by the second foreign key that links `mentee_id` in the **mentorships** table with `id` in the **employees** table.

Recall that the second foreign key has a `ON UPDATE CASCADE` clause? This means that any update in the parent table (**employees**) will lead to a corresponding update in the child table (**mentorships**).

We can verify that using the two statements below:

```
SELECT * FROM employees;
SELECT * FROM mentorships;
```

The `SELECT` keyword is used to retrieve information from tables. We'll learn more about that in the next three chapters. For now, try executing the statements above. You should get the following outputs.

id	em_name	gender	contact_n...	salary	years_in_co...	date_created
1	James Lee	M	516-514-1...	3500	11	2007-09-21 11:20:46
2	Peter Pasternak	M	845-644-7...	6010	10	2008-09-12 22:23:20
3	Clara Couto	F	845-641-5...	3900	8	2010-11-01 16:13:45
6	Joyce Jones	F	523-172-2...	8000	3	2015-06-22 12:21:46
7	Jason Cerrone	M	725-441-7...	7980	2	2016-01-25 15:22:16
8	Prudence Phelps	F	546-312-5...	11000	2	2016-09-12 12:20:22
9	Larry Zucker	M	817-267-9...	3500	1	2017-03-12 11:18:16
10	Serena Parker	F	621-211-7...	12000	1	2017-10-18 18:14:23
11	Walker Welch	M	NULL	2500	4	2014-10-30 13:41:23

mentor_id	mentee_id	status	project
1	2	Ongoing	SQF Limited
1	3	Past	Wayne Fibre
2	3	Ongoing	SQF Limited
3	11	Ongoing	SQF Limited

Note that as the date_created column in the **employees** table is provided by the NOW() function, the values that you get for that column will be different from those values shown above. The values that you get will be based on the time you created the record.

As you can see, the id for Walker Welch in the **employees** table is updated from 4 to 11. This update is cascaded to the **mentorships** table. The mentee_id for the last row in the **mentorships** table is changed from 4 to 11 too.

Clear about how the ON UPDATE CASCADE clause works?

Good!

Last but not least, let's look at the ON DELETE CASCADE clause. We added this clause to both our foreign keys.

Recall that previously, we deleted 'Li Xiao Ting' from the **employees** table?

If you study the **employees** table above, you'll notice that the row with id = 5 is missing.

In addition, if you compare the **mentorships** table above with the data that we inserted into this table, you'll see that the last row is deleted too.

This is due to the ON DELETE CASCADE clause that we added to our foreign keys. The last row has mentee_id = 5. Hence, it is deleted from the **mentorships** table (the child table) when the referenced row is deleted from the parent table (the **employees** table).

Chapter 5: Selecting Data Part 1

In this chapter, we'll learn to select data from our database. This is a relatively large topic, so we'll be splitting it into three chapters.

The data used for selection are from the two tables (**employees** and **mentorships**) that we created in the previous chapters. These tables can be found in Appendix A for easy reference.

In the first chapter, we'll learn to select data from a single table.

Basic Select Syntax

To select data from a single table, we use the syntax

```
SELECT column_names_or_other_information
[AS alias]
[ORDER BY column(s)] [DESC]
FROM table_name
[WHERE condition];
```

Let's look at some examples.

Selecting Everything

If we want to select all the columns and rows from a table, we write

```
SELECT * FROM table_name;
```

For instance, as we saw in the previous chapter, to select all data from the **employees** table, we write

```
SELECT * FROM employees;
```

In the statement above, we did not add a `WHERE` clause. Without the `WHERE` clause, MySQL gives us all the rows in the table.

In addition, we used the * symbol to indicate that we want to select all columns from the **employees** table.

Filtering Columns

If we do not want to select all columns, we can list the columns we want.

Suppose we only want to select the `em_name` and `gender` columns from the **employees** table, we write

SELECT em_name, gender from employees;

The table below shows part of the results from this `SELECT` statement:

em_name	gender
James Lee	M
Peter Pasternak	M
Clara Couto	F
Joyce Jones	F

Using Aliases

If you study the table above, you'll notice that the table uses the column names ("em_name" and "gender") as its column headings.

If we want the column heading to display a different name instead, we can use an alias for the column.

We do that using the `AS` keyword as shown in the following statement:

SELECT em_name AS `Employee Name`, gender AS Gender FROM employees;

In the statement above, note that we use the backtick character (normally found at the top left corner of the keyboard, together with the tilde ~ character) to enclose the first alias "Employee Name". This is necessary when the alias consists of more than one word. Alternatively, we can also use single or double quotes as shown below:

```
SELECT em_name AS "Employee Name", gender AS Gender
FROM employees;
```

or

```
SELECT em_name AS 'Employee Name', gender AS Gender
FROM employees;
```

If you run any of the statements above, you'll see the heading change from "em_name" and "gender" to "Employee Name" and "Gender" respectively.

Filtering Rows

Next, let's look at how we can filter rows when selecting data.

LIMIT

To do that, we can use the LIMIT keyword. This limits the number of rows retrieved by the SELECT statement. For instance, if we write

```
SELECT em_name AS 'Employee Name', gender AS Gender
FROM employees LIMIT 3;
```

we'll get

Employee Name	Gender
James Lee	M
Peter Pasternak	M
Clara Couto	F

Only the first three rows are displayed.

DISTINCT

Another way to filter rows is to remove duplicates. This can be achieved using the DISTINCT keyword.

If we write

SELECT gender FROM employees;

we'll get

```
M
M
F
F
M
F
M
F
M
```

as the output.

This means that the first two rows in our table have gender = M while the third and fourth rows have gender = F etc.

If we want to remove the duplicates, we can write

SELECT DISTINCT(gender) FROM employees;

We'll get

```
M
F
```

as the output.

WHERE clause

Next, let's look at how we can use the WHERE clause to filter results.

We've already seen the WHERE clause in the previous chapter when we used the statement

```
UPDATE employees
SET contact_number = '516-514-1729'
WHERE id = 1;
```

to update the contact number of the employee with an id of 1 (WHERE id = 1).

In that example, we used the equality (=) operator in the WHERE clause. Besides the equality operator, there are other operators and keywords that we can use:

Comparison

We can do a comparison between two values using the following operators:

Not Equal (!=), Greater than (>), Greater than or equal to (>=), Smaller than (<), Smaller than or equal to (<=)

For instance, if we want to select all rows from the **employees** table whose id is not equal to 1, we write

```
SELECT * FROM employees WHERE id != 1;
```

Between

Besides using mathematical operators, we can also use different keywords in the WHERE clause.

If we want to select rows with values between two numbers, we can use the BETWEEN keyword. For instance, to select rows with id between 1 (inclusive) and 3 (inclusive), we write

```
SELECT * FROM employees WHERE id BETWEEN 1 AND 3;
```

Like

If we want to select rows whose column values "look like" a specified pattern, we use the LIKE keyword.

If we want to select employees whose names end with 'er', we can do it as follows:

```
SELECT * FROM employees WHERE em_name LIKE '%er';
```

The % symbol is used to indicate that there can be an unknown number of characters in front of 'er'.

If you run the statement above, you'll get the records of Larry Zucker and Serena Parker. This is because both names end with 'er'.

If we want to select employees whose names have 'er' anywhere within (not necessarily at the back), we can use the following statement:

```
SELECT * FROM employees WHERE em_name LIKE '%er%';
```

We add the % symbol in front of and behind 'er' to indicate that there can be any number of characters before and after it.

If you run the statement above, you'll get the records of all 5 employees with 'er' in their names (`Peter Pasternak`, `Jason Cerrone`, `Larry Zucker`, `Serena Parker` and `Walker Welch`).

Besides the `%` symbol, MySQL also provides us with the `_` symbol.

In contrast to the `%` symbol that represents an unknown number of characters, the `_` symbol is used to represent exactly ONE character.

Suppose we want to select the rows of all employees that have 'e' as the fifth letter in their names, we write:

`SELECT * FROM employees WHERE em_name LIKE '____e%';`

Here, we use FOUR `_` symbols to indicate that there are four characters before 'e'. This will give us the records of `Joyce Jones`, `Prudence Phelps` and `Walker Welch`.

In

Next, let's look at the `IN` keyword.

This keyword is used to select rows with column values inside a certain list. Suppose we want to select rows that have `id` 6, 7, or 9, we can write

`SELECT * FROM employees WHERE id IN (6, 7, 9);`

Not in

On the other hand, if we want to select rows that <u>do not</u> have `id` 7 or 8, we use the `NOT IN` keywords:

`SELECT * FROM employees WHERE id NOT IN (7, 8);`

Note that in both examples above, we need to enclose the ids inside a pair of parentheses.

And, Or

Finally, let's look at the AND and OR keywords. These keywords are used to combine conditions in the WHERE clause.

The AND keyword gives us rows that satisfy ALL the conditions listed while the OR keyword selects rows that satisfy at least one of the conditions.

We can use parentheses to indicate which conditions should be combined first.

For instance, if we want to select all female employees who have worked more than 5 years in the company or have salaries above 5000, we can write:

SELECT * FROM employees WHERE (years_in_company > 5 OR salary > 5000) AND gender = 'F';

This gives us the following output:

id	em_name	gender	contact_n...	salary	years_in_co...	date_created
3	Clara Couto	F	845-641-5...	3900	8	2010-11-01 16:13:45
6	Joyce Jones	F	523-172-2...	8000	3	2015-06-22 12:21:46
8	Prudence Phelps	F	546-312-5...	11000	2	2016-09-12 12:20:22
10	Serena Parker	F	621-211-7...	12000	1	2017-10-18 18:14:23

Clara Couto is selected even though her income is only 3900. This is because she has worked 8 years in the company. Hence, she satisfies the first of the two OR conditions inside the parentheses (years_in_company > 5 OR salary > 5000).

The OR keyword requires employees to satisfy at least one of the conditions.

On the other hand, if you study the **employees** table, you'll see that some employees are not selected even though they also satisfy at least one OR condition in the parentheses.

For instance, `James Lee` has worked 11 years in the company but is not selected.

This is due to the `AND` keyword that requires `James Lee` to not only satisfy the

```
years_in_company > 5 OR salary > 5000
```

condition (which he does), but to also satisfy the

```
gender = 'F'
```

condition (which he doesn't).

Clear?

Subqueries

Next, let's look at subqueries.

Subqueries are commonly used to filter the results of one table based on the results of a query on another table.

For instance, in our example, suppose we want to select the names of all employees that are mentors of the `'SQF Limited'` project.

We can select them using their ids. If we know that employee 1, 2 and 3 are mentors of this project, we can use the following `SELECT` statement:

```
SELECT em_name from employees WHERE id IN (1, 2, 3);
```

However, what if we do not know their ids?

What we can do is use a subquery in the `WHERE` clause to get their ids first. This can be achieved with the statement below:

```
SELECT em_name from employees WHERE id IN
(SELECT mentor_id FROM mentorships WHERE project =
'SQF Limited');
```

Here, we replace

```
(1, 2, 3)
```

with

```
(SELECT mentor_id FROM mentorships WHERE project =
'SQF Limited')
```

This query is known as a subquery. We use this subquery to get the ids from the **mentorships** table first. We then use this result in the WHERE clause of the main query to get the em_name column values from the **employees** table.

If you run the main query (in bold) above, you'll get James Lee, Peter Pasternak and Clara Couto as the result.

Sorting Rows

Now that we know how to select data from our tables and filter the results, let's cover one last concept before we end this chapter. Let's look at how we can sort the results returned by the SELECT statement.

To do that, we use the ORDER BY clause. We can choose to sort the results based on one or more columns.

Suppose we want to sort the rows of the **employees** table using gender, followed by the employee's name (em_name), we write

```
SELECT * FROM employees ORDER BY gender, em_name;
```

This results in the records of female employees being displayed first, followed by male employees (since the letter F comes before M).

Within each gender, the records will be sorted by the employees' names.

Note that the default sorting order is ascending. If we want to sort by descending order, we use the DESC keyword as shown below:

```
SELECT * FROM employees ORDER BY gender DESC,
em_name;
```

This results in the records of male employees being displayed first.

Chapter 6: Selecting Data Part 2

In the previous chapter, we learned quite a few keywords that we can use to select data from our tables.

In this chapter, we'll learn to use built-in functions in our `SELECT` statements.

What is a Function?

First off, what is a function?

A function is a block of code that does a certain job for us. For an analogy, think of the mathematical functions available in MS Excel. To add numbers, we can use the `sum()` function and type `sum(A1:A5)` instead of typing `A1+A2+A3+A4+A5`.

A function in MySQL is similar; it helps us accomplish certain tasks more easily.

MySQL provides us with a large number of pre-written functions that we can use in our SQL statements.

The full list of MySQL functions can be found at
https://dev.mysql.com/doc/refman/8.0/en/func-op-summary-ref.html

Let's look at some of them in this chapter.

MySQL Functions

The first two functions that we'll look at are for working with strings.

CONCAT()

The first is the CONCAT() function. This function allows us to combine two or more strings into a single string. This is known as concatenating the strings.

To use the CONCAT() function, we need to provide it with some input. Specifically, we need to tell the function what strings to concatenate.

For instance, if we want to concatenate 'Hello' and ' World', we write

```
CONCAT('Hello', ' World');
```

To display the result of this function, we use the SELECT keyword.

Besides using the SELECT keyword to select information from tables, we can also use it to display messages.

Try running the statement below:

```
SELECT CONCAT('Hello', ' World');
```

You'll get

```
Hello World
```

as the output.

SUBSTRING()

Another commonly used function is the SUBSTRING() function. This function allows us to extract a substring from a specified string. A substring refers to a portion of a longer string.

The SUBSTRING() function requires us to pass in a string, the starting position to extract the substring, and the desired length of the substring (in that order). If the desired length is not specified, the function extracts from the starting position to the end of the string.

For instance,

```
SELECT SUBSTRING('Programming', 2);
```

gives us

```
rogramming
```

as we extract the substring starting from position 2 to the end of the string.

On the other hand,

```
SELECT SUBSTRING('Programming', 2, 6);
```

gives us

```
rogram
```

which is a substring that starts from position 2, with a length of 6 characters.

Besides functions for manipulating strings, we also have functions for working with date and time.

NOW()

One such function is the NOW() function that we learned in Chapter 3. This function gives us the current date and time whenever that function is being used. It is commonly used to record the date and time that a particular record is inserted into a table.

CURDATE()

Next, we have the CURDATE() function. This gives us the current date.

For instance,

```
SELECT CURDATE();
```

gives me

```
2018-08-28
```

at the time of writing.

CURTIME()

Finally, we have the CURTIME() function. This gives us the current time.

Aggregate Functions

Besides the functions mentioned above, MySQL also comes with a large number of pre-written aggregate functions.

An aggregate function is a function that performs calculation on a set of values and returns the result of the calculation as a single value.

We can use some of these built-in aggregate functions to perform various calculations on the data in our tables.

Let's look at some of these functions and apply them on our **employees** table.

The calculations below are based on the **employees** table found in Appendix A.

The commonly used aggregate functions in MySQL include:

COUNT()

The COUNT() function returns the number of the rows in the table.

If we pass in * to the function, it returns the total number of rows in the table.

If we pass in a column name instead, it returns the number of non NULL values in that column (NULL values are ignored).

If we want to remove duplicates, we add the DISTINCT keyword before the column name.

Example 1:
`SELECT COUNT(*) FROM employees;`

Result:
9

Example 2:
`SELECT COUNT(contact_number) FROM employees;`

Result:
8

The last row (Walker Welch) is excluded from the count as the value is NULL.

Example 3a:
`SELECT COUNT(gender) FROM employees;`

Result:
9

Example 3b:
`SELECT COUNT(DISTINCT gender) FROM employees;`

Result:
2

AVG()

The AVG() function returns the average of a set of values.

Example:
```
SELECT AVG(salary) FROM employees;
```

Result:
```
6487.777777777777
```

If you want to format the output, you can use the ROUND() function. We need to pass in two pieces of information to the ROUND() function - the number to round off and the number of decimal places we want it rounded off to.

For instance,

```
SELECT ROUND(1.23456, 3);
```

gives us 1.235.

In our case, if we want to round off the result of the AVG() function to 2 decimal places, we write

```
SELECT ROUND(AVG(salary), 2) FROM employees;
```

We'll get 6487.78.

MAX()

The MAX() function returns the maximum of a set of values.

Example:
```
SELECT MAX(salary) FROM employees;
```

Result:
```
12000
```

MIN()

The MIN() function returns the minimum of a set of values.

Example:
```
SELECT MIN(salary) FROM employees;
```

Result:
```
2500
```

SUM()

The SUM() function returns the sum of a set of values.

Example:
```
SELECT SUM(salary) FROM employees;
```

Result:
```
58390
```

GROUP BY

In the previous section, we learned to use aggregate functions to perform calculations on our data. However, those calculations were performed on all the values in the column. What if we are interested in the maximum salary of males vs females?

MySQL allows us to group data when performing calculations. For instance, we can ask MySQL to group the data based on gender and perform the calculation on the two groups separately. To do that, we use the GROUP BY clause:

```
SELECT gender, MAX(salary) FROM employees GROUP BY
gender;
```

That'll give us the following output:

gender	MAX(salary)
M	7980
F	12000

HAVING

In addition to performing calculations on grouped data, we can also filter the results of the grouped data. We do that using the HAVING clause.

Suppose we want to display rows from the previous table only when the maximum salary is above 10000, we do that using the statement below:

```
SELECT gender, MAX(salary) FROM employees GROUP BY
gender HAVING MAX(salary) > 10000;
```

That'll remove the first row from the previous table.

Chapter 7: Selecting Data Part 3

We've covered quite a few data selection concepts in the last two chapters. Those two chapters focused mainly on selecting data from a single table.

In this chapter, we'll learn to select and combine data from one or more tables.

Joins

Let's start with joins.

Like the name suggests, a join is used to join data from different tables based on a related column between the tables.

The syntax for joining two tables is:

```
SELECT
[table_names.]columns_names_or_other_information
FROM
left_table
JOIN / INNER JOIN / LEFT JOIN / RIGHT JOIN
right_table
ON
left_table.column_name = right_table.column_name;
```

There are three main types of joins in MySQL: inner join, left join and right join. These are represented by the Venn diagrams below:

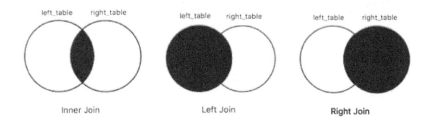

| | left_table | right_table | | left_table | right_table | | left_table | right_table |
| Inner Join | | | Left Join | | | Right Join | | |

To demonstrate the difference between them, let's consider the following two tables:

A	B
1	259
2	125
3	731

Table Name: one

C	B	D
2	218.1	ABC
3	511.5	DEF
4	219.9	GHI

Table Name: two

Here, we have two tables called **one** and **two**.

You can see that column A in table **one** shares some common values with column C in table **two**. We can join the two tables using these two columns.

If we do an inner join, we write

```
SELECT A, C, one.B AS 'one B', two.B AS 'two B'
FROM
one
INNER JOIN
two
ON
A = C;
```

There are a few points to note about this SELECT statement.

Firstly, in the statement above, table **one** is the left table while table **two** is the right table. The left table refers to the first table mentioned after the FROM keyword.

Secondly, the JOIN condition used is A = C.

Thirdly, for some of the columns (specifically column B), we need to prefix the column name with a table name (such as one.B, two.B etc). This is done to avoid ambiguity as there is a column B in both tables **one** and **two**. If we do not include the table name, MySQL will not know which table we want to get the values from. If we want, we can also prefix the other columns with their table names, such as one.A and two.C. However, that is optional as columns A and C are not ambiguous.

Lastly, an inner join is the default join. In the statement above, we could have omitted the INNER keyword.

If you create the two tables yourself and run the SELECT statement above, you'll get the following output:

A	C	one B	two B
2	2	125	218.1
3	3	731	511.5

If you study the output carefully, you'll notice that <u>an inner join selects rows where a common value exists for both tables</u>. Hence, only A=2 and A=3 are selected from table **one** as these two values (2 and 3) exist in column C of table **two** as well.

Clear?

Good!

Let's move on to a left join.

To do a left join, we simply replace `INNER JOIN` with `LEFT JOIN` in the previous SQL statement. That will give us the following output:

A	C	one B	two B
2	2	125	218.1
3	3	731	511.5
1	NULL	259	NULL

A left join selects all rows from the left table as shown in the output above.

As the two tables are joined using the condition $A = C$ and table **two** (the right table) does not have a row with $C = 1$, the values for table **two** are displayed as `NULL` when A=1 (refer to the last row in the results table above).

Finally, let's do a right join. A right join selects all rows from the right table.

To do a right join, we replace `LEFT JOIN` with `RIGHT JOIN` in the SQL statement. This will give us the following output:

A	C	one B	two B
2	2	125	218.1
3	3	731	511.5
NULL	4	NULL	219.9

As table **one** (the left table) does not have a row with $A = 4$, the values for table **one** are displayed as `NULL` for that row.

Clear?

Great!

Now, let's look at an example using our **employees** and **mentorships** tables.

Type the following code into *practice.sql* and execute it:

```
SELECT employees.id, mentorships.mentor_id,
employees.em_name AS 'Mentor', mentorships.project AS
'Project Name'
FROM
mentorships
JOIN
employees
ON
employees.id = mentorships.mentor_id;
```

You'll get the following output:

id	mentor_id	Mentor	Project Name
1	1	James Lee	SQF Limited
1	1	James Lee	Wayne Fibre
2	2	Peter Pasternak	SQF Limited
3	3	Clara Couto	SQF Limited

Study the output carefully to fully appreciate how a join works.

In the example above, if you do not want the `id` and `mentor_id` columns to show, you can use the code below:

```
SELECT employees.em_name AS 'Mentor',
mentorships.project AS 'Project Name'
FROM
mentorships
JOIN
employees
ON
employees.id = mentorships.mentor_id;
```

You do not have to select the columns that you use for joining. The statement above gives us the same rows but without the `id` and `mentor_id` columns.

Unions

Now that we understand how joins work, let's move on to unions. This is a relatively easy concept.

The `UNION` keyword is used to combine the results of two or more `SELECT` statements. Each `SELECT` statement must have the same number of columns. The syntax is:

```
SELECT_statement_one
UNION
SELECT_statement_two;
```

The column names from the first `SELECT` statement will be used as the column names for the results returned.

Let's look at an example.

For the **employees** table, we can do a `UNION` as follows:

```
SELECT em_name, salary FROM employees WHERE gender = 'M'
UNION
SELECT em_name, years_in_company FROM employees WHERE gender = 'F';
```

We'll get the following output:

em_name	salary
James Lee	3500
Peter Pasternak	6010
Jason Cerrone	7980
Larry Zucker	3500
Walker Welch	2500
Clara Couto	8
Joyce Jones	3
Prudence Phelps	2
Serena Parker	1

The first 5 rows are from the first SELECT statement while the last 4 are from the second statement.

Note that by default, the UNION keyword removes any duplicates from the result. If you do not want that to happen, you can use the UNION ALL keywords.

For instance, if we do a UNION ALL as follows

```
SELECT mentor_id FROM mentorships
UNION ALL
SELECT id FROM employees WHERE gender = 'F';
```

we'll get 1, 1, 2, 3, 3, 6, 8, 10 as the result. The ids 1 and 3 are repeated because they are returned by both SELECT statements.

In contrast, if we simply do a UNION, we'll get 1, 2, 3, 6, 8, 10 as the result. The duplicates are removed.

Chapter 8: Views

In the last three chapters, we learned to write some pretty complex SELECT statements to get information from our databases.

In this chapter, we'll learn another concept that is closely related to SELECT statements - the concept of views.

What is a view?

Simply stated, an SQL view is a **virtual table**.

In contrast to actual tables, views do not contain data. Instead, they contain SELECT statements. The data to display is retrieved using those SELECT statements.

One advantage of using views is that it allows programmers to simplify their code. They can write relatively complex SELECT statements to join multiple tables into a single virtual table. Once that is done, they can access that virtual table like a normal table and perform simple searches on it.

In addition, views also allow us to restrict access to certain data in our tables. For instance, suppose we have a table with three columns - id, password and email. If we do not want other programmers to have access to all the data in the tables (such as the password column), we can create a view with only the id and email columns and let them have access to the view instead.

Creating a View

The syntax for creating a view is:

```
CREATE VIEW name_of_view AS
SELECT statement;
```

Quite straightforward, right?

Let's look at an example.

In the previous chapter, we wrote a SELECT statement to join the **employees** table with the **mentorships** table.

The code below shows how we can create a view for that SELECT statement:

```
CREATE VIEW myView AS
SELECT employees.id, mentorships.mentor_id,
employees.em_name AS 'Mentor', mentorships.project AS
'Project Name'
FROM
mentorships
JOIN
employees
ON
employees.id = mentorships.mentor_id;
```

The only additional code is the first line (CREATE VIEW myView AS).

To use this view, we need to first execute the CREATE VIEW statement above to create the view.

Next, we can select data from it like how we select data from a table.

For instance, we can write

```
SELECT * FROM myView;
```

to view all the data.

If we only want the `mentor_id` and `Project Name` columns, we can write

```
SELECT mentor_id, `Project Name` FROM myView;
```

Note that in the SELECT statement above, we have to enclose `Project Name` using the backtick (` ` `) character. If we use single or double quotes as shown below:

```
SELECT mentor_id, 'Project Name' FROM myView;
```

we'll get the following results, which is obviously not what we want.

mentor_id	Project Name
1	Project Name
1	Project Name
2	Project Name
3	Project Name

Single or double quotes can only be used when naming the alias for the column. For selecting the column, we have to use backticks.

Altering a View

After creating a view, if we want to make any changes to it, we use the ALTER VIEW keywords.

The syntax is

```
ALTER VIEW name_of_view AS
SELECT statement;
```

For instance, we can use the following statement to alter `myView`:

```
ALTER VIEW myView AS
SELECT employees.id, mentorships.mentor_id,
employees.em_name AS 'Mentor', mentorships.project AS
'Project'
FROM
mentorships
JOIN
employees
ON
employees.id = mentorships.mentor_id;
```

This changes the alias for the mentorships.project column from Project Name to Project (refer to underlined code).

Deleting a View

Last but not least, to delete a view, we use the DROP VIEW keywords. The syntax is

```
DROP VIEW [IF EXISTS] name_of_view;
```

To delete myView, we write

```
DROP VIEW IF EXISTS myView;
```

Chapter 9: Triggers

In this chapter, we'll talk about another interesting feature in MySQL - triggers.

What is a Trigger?

A trigger is a series of actions that is activated when a defined event occurs for a specific table. This event can either be an INSERT, UPDATE or DELETE. Triggers can be invoked before or after the event.

To understand how triggers work, let's look at an example.

We'll use the **employees** table to demonstrate.

Suppose one of the employees has just resigned from the company and we want to delete this employee from the **employees** table. However, before we do that, we would like to transfer the data into another table called **ex_employees** as a form of back up. We can do this using a trigger.

Let's first create an **ex_employees** table using the code below:

```
CREATE TABLE ex_employees (
    em_id INT PRIMARY KEY,
    em_name VARCHAR(255) NOT NULL,
    gender CHAR(1) NOT NULL,
    date_left TIMESTAMP DEFAULT NOW()
);
```

Creating a Trigger

Next, we'll use the following syntax to create our trigger (line numbers are added on the left for reference and are not part of the syntax):

```
1 DELIMITER $$
2
3 CREATE TRIGGER name_of_trigger BEFORE/AFTER
UPDATE/DELETE/INSERT ON name_of_table FOR EACH ROW
4
5 BEGIN
6 -- Actions to take
7 END $$
8
9 DELIMITER ;
```

This syntax may look overwhelming at first. Do not worry, we'll go over each keyword one by one.

On line 1, we have a new keyword - DELIMITER.

A delimiter is a character or sequence of characters that specifies the end of a SQL statement. Recall that previously, we have always used ; to specify the end of our SQL statements? We can change that if we want.

The code on line 1 (DELIMITER $$) tells MySQL that we want to use $$ as the delimiter for our CREATE TRIGGER statement (from lines 3 to 7).

Why do we need to do that?

The reason for this is that a trigger contains SQL statements within itself. We use the ; character to signify the end of those SQL statements inside the trigger and use the $$ characters to signify the end of the trigger itself.

We could have used other characters as the delimiter, but it is customary to use $$.

We change the delimiter back to ; on line 9.

Using $$ as the delimiter is necessary only for statements that contain SQL statements within itself (such as the CREATE TRIGGER and CREATE PROCEDURE statements that we'll cover in the next chapter).

Clear?

Good! Let's move on to the actual trigger.

The actual trigger is created on line 3 using the CREATE TRIGGER keywords.

Each trigger must be associated with a table. We use ON name_of_table to link the trigger to the table.

Finally, the keywords FOR EACH ROW is standard syntax to inform MySQL that this trigger is to be activated for each of the rows affected by the UPDATE, INSERT or DELETE event.

After line 3, we have the BEGIN and END $$ markers on lines 5 and 7. These two markers mark the beginning and end of the trigger. Between these two markers, we insert the SQL statements that define the actions to take.

Let's look at an actual example. As mentioned previously, we want to create a trigger that inserts the record of an employee into a new table called **ex_employees** before we delete the record from the **employees** table. We do that using the code below:

```
DELIMITER $$

CREATE TRIGGER update_ex_employees BEFORE DELETE ON
employees FOR EACH ROW
BEGIN
   INSERT INTO ex_employees (em_id, em_name, gender)
VALUES (OLD.id, OLD.em_name, OLD.gender);
END $$

DELIMITER ;
```

The name of the trigger is `update_ex_employees`.

We use `BEFORE DELETE ON employees` to indicate that we want this trigger to be activated before we delete the record from the **employees** table. If we want the trigger to be activated after we delete the record, we'll write `AFTER DELETE ON employees`.

Next, within the `BEGIN` and `END $$` markers, we have an `INSERT` statement to insert a new row into the **ex_employees** table. This `INSERT` statement should be quite familiar to you, except for the `OLD` keyword.

For triggers activated by a `DELETE` event, we use the `OLD` keyword to retrieve the deleted values (or values to be deleted).

For triggers activated by an `INSERT` event, we use the `NEW` keyword to retrieve the inserted data (or data to be inserted).

For triggers activated by an `UPDATE` event, we use the `OLD` keyword to retrieve the original data, and the `NEW` keyword to retrieve the updated data.

To get a feel of how triggers work, type the trigger above into *practice.sql* and execute it. Next, execute the statements below:

```
DELETE FROM employees WHERE id = 10;

SELECT * FROM employees;
SELECT * FROM ex_employees;
```

We first delete employee 10 from the **employees** table. Next, we retrieve data from both the **employees** and **ex_employees** tables.

You'll see that employee 10 is removed from the **employees** table and a new row is added to the **ex_employees** table automatically. Cool right?

Deleting a Trigger

Finally, let's look at how we can delete an existing trigger.

To do that, we use the following syntax:

```
DROP TRIGGER [IF EXISTS] name_of_trigger;
```

To drop our `update_ex_employees` trigger, we write

```
DROP TRIGGER IF EXISTS update_ex_employees;
```

Chapter 10: Variables and Stored Routines

Congratulations on making it this far! We've covered most of the fundamental concepts in SQL.

In this chapter, we'll cover something more advanced. Specifically, we'll talk about stored routines.

However, before we do that, let's first discuss variables. We need to understand variables before we can fully appreciate stored routines.

Variables

So what is a variable?

A variable is a name given to data that we need to store and use in our SQL statements.

For instance, suppose we want to get all information related to employee 1 from the **employees** and **mentorships** tables. We can do that as follows:

```
SELECT * FROM employees WHERE id = 1;
SELECT * FROM mentorships WHERE mentor_id = 1;
SELECT * FROM mentorships WHERE mentee_id = 1;
```

However, if we realize that we made a mistake and want the information of employee 2 instead, we'll have to change all the three SQL statements above. This is relatively easy for three statements, but can be a lot of trouble if there are hundreds of statements. A better way is to use variables.

To do that, we can first declare and initialize a variable using the statement below:

```
SET @em_id = 1;
```

Here, we declare a variable called @em_id. User defined variables in MySQL have to be prefixed with the @ symbol.

In addition, we assign a value of 1 to the variable using the SET keyword. This is known as initializing the variable (i.e. giving it an initial value). We can always change the value of the variable later.

Once the variable is declared and initialized, we can modify our SELECT statements to make use of this variable:

```
SELECT * FROM mentorships WHERE mentor_id = @em_id;
SELECT * FROM mentorships WHERE mentee_id = @em_id;
SELECT * FROM employees WHERE id = @em_id;
```

In the modified statements above, we simply replaced 1 in the original statements with @em_id.

In order to get the data for employee 1 now, we have to execute the SET statement and the three SELECT statements.

Subsequently, if we need to get the information for other employees, we can assign another value to @em_id and run the statements again. For instance, to get the information for employee 2, we can assign a new value to @em_id using the statement below:

```
SET @em_id = 2;
```

We can then execute this SET statement and re-execute the SELECT statements. We'll get the information for employee 2. There is no need to change any of the SELECT statements.

Clear?

Variables make it very easy for us to reuse our SQL statements and are extremely useful in stored routines. We'll cover stored routines in the next section.

Before that, let's cover a few more concepts related to variables.

Besides assigning numerical values to variables, we can also assign text to them. To do that, we need to use quotation marks:

```
SET @em_name = 'Jamie';
```

Next, we can assign the result of a mathematical operation to a variable. For instance, we can do the following:

```
SET @price = 12;
SET @price = @price + 3;
```

In the first SET statement, we declare a variable called @price and initialize it to 12.

In the second SET statement, we update the value of @price by adding 3 to it.

SET statements always work from right to left (i.e. the right side of the statement is executed first).

In other words, 3 is added to the original value of @price first.

The result is then assigned back to @price.

The value of @price thus becomes 15.

Last but not least, we can assign the result of a function to a variable.

For instance, we can do the following:

```
SET @result = SQRT(9);
```

Here, we assign the result of the `SQRT()` function to `@result`.

`SQRT()` is a pre-written function in MySQL that gives us the square root of a number. In the statement above, `SQRT(9)` gives 3 as the answer. This value is then assigned to `@result`.

To verify that, we can display the value of `@result`.

In order to display the value of any variable, we use the `SELECT` keyword.

Try running the statements below:

```
SET @result = SQRT(9);
SELECT @result;
```

You'll get 3 as the result.

Alternatively, we can combine the two statements into a single statement:

```
SELECT @result := SQRT(9);
```

That is, we can combine a `SET` statement with a `SELECT` statement.

However, if you choose to do that, you have to use the `:=` symbol to do the assignment in the `SELECT` statement. The `=` symbol will not work correctly.

If you run the statement above, you'll get 3 as the result too.

Stored Routines

Next, let's move on to stored routines.

A stored routine is a set of SQL statements that are grouped, named and stored together in the server. Do not worry if this does not make much sense to you at the moment. We'll discuss it in greater depth later.

There are two types of stored routines - stored procedures and stored functions.

Stored Procedures

Let's first look at stored procedures.

We can create a stored procedure using the syntax below:

```
DELIMITER $$

CREATE PROCEDURE name_of_procedure([parameters, if
any])
BEGIN
    -- SQL Statements
END $$

DELIMITER ;
```

Most of the syntax is pretty similar to the syntax for creating a trigger.

The main difference is, instead of using CREATE TRIGGER, we use CREATE PROCEDURE to create the stored procedure.

In addition, we have a pair of parentheses after the CREATE PROCEDURE keywords.

These parentheses allow us to pass values to our stored procedure using a special type of variable known as parameters. Parameters are optional; we'll discuss them in the second example.

For now, let's first look at a simple example on creating a procedure without parameters.

Suppose we want to create a stored procedure to select all information from our two tables (**employees** and **mentorships**).

Here's how we do it:

```
DELIMITER $$

CREATE PROCEDURE select_info()
BEGIN
   SELECT * FROM employees;
   SELECT * FROM mentorships;
END $$

DELIMITER ;
```

We first change the delimiter to $$. Next, we use the CREATE PROCEDURE keywords to create the stored procedure.

The name of the stored procedure is select_info. We need to add a pair of parentheses after the name. A pair of empty parentheses indicates that this stored procedure has no parameters.

After the BEGIN keyword, we add two SELECT statements to the stored procedure. Next, we end the stored procedure with END $$.

Finally, we change the delimiter back to a semi-colon (;).

Pretty straightforward, right?

Try typing the stored procedure into *practice.sql* yourself and execute it to create the procedure. We always need to execute the CREATE PROCEDURE statement to create our procedures before we can use them.

Next, let's run this stored procedure. To do that, we use the CALL keyword:

```
CALL select_info();
```

If you execute the statement above, you'll see the **employees** and **mentorships** tables displayed in two separate tabs in the results grid.

Got it?

Great!

Let's move on to a more advanced example.

Suppose instead of selecting everything from the two tables, we only want to select the records of a particular employee. We can create a stored procedure as follows:

```
DELIMITER $$

CREATE PROCEDURE employee_info(IN p_em_id INT)
BEGIN
    SELECT * FROM mentorships WHERE mentor_id =
p_em_id;
    SELECT * FROM mentorships WHERE mentee_id =
p_em_id;
    SELECT * FROM employees WHERE id = p_em_id;
END $$

DELIMITER ;
```

Most of the code should be familiar to you. The only exception is the code inside the parentheses:

```
IN p_em_id INT
```

Here, we declare a variable called p_em_id. You may notice that we did not prefix this variable with @.

This is because the variable here is a special type of variable known as a parameter. Parameters are variables that we use to pass information to, or get information from, our stored routines. We do not prefix parameters with @.

There are three types of parameters for stored procedures: IN, OUT and INOUT.

An IN parameter is used to pass information to the stored procedure.

An OUT parameter is used to get information from the stored procedure while an INOUT parameter serves as both an IN and OUT parameter.

We'll look at OUT and INOUT parameters in the next few examples.

For now, let's focus on the IN parameter. To declare an IN parameter, we use the IN keyword followed by the parameter name (p_em_id) and data type (INT).

Once we declare this IN parameter, we can use it in our SQL statements within the stored procedure. In our example, we used it in the WHERE clause of all the three SELECT statements.

In order to call this stored procedure, we need to pass in a value to the IN parameter.

Suppose we want to get the information for employee 1, we write:

```
CALL employee_info(1);
```

Here, we pass in the value 1 to the stored procedure. This tells MySQL that the value of p_em_id should be replaced by 1 in all the SQL statements within the stored procedure.

For instance, the statement

```
SELECT * FROM employees WHERE id = p_em_id;
```

becomes

```
SELECT * FROM employees WHERE id = 1;
```

The three `SELECT` statements will then only select information for employee 1.

Clear?

Next, let's look at an example for `OUT` parameters. Suppose we want to get the name and gender of a particular employee. In addition, we want to store these information into variables so that we can use them in our subsequent SQL statements. Here's how we can do it:

```
DELIMITER $$

CREATE PROCEDURE employee_name_gender(IN p_em_id INT,
OUT p_name VARCHAR(255), OUT p_gender CHAR(1))
BEGIN
   SELECT em_name, gender INTO p_name, p_gender FROM
employees WHERE id = p_em_id;
END $$

DELIMITER ;
```

Here, we declare an `IN` parameter called `p_em_id` and two `OUT` parameters called `p_name` and `p_gender`.

Inside the stored procedure, we use the `INTO` keyword to store the results returned by the SQL statement into the `OUT` parameters.

To call the stored procedure, we write

```
CALL employee_name_gender(1, @v_name, @v_gender);
```

Inside the parentheses, we pass the value 1 to the `IN` parameter and the variables `@v_name` and `@v_gender` to the `OUT` parameters.

You may notice that we did not declare @v_name and @v_gender before passing them to our stored procedure. This is allowed in MySQL. When we pass in variables that have not been declared previously, MySQL will declare the variables for us. Hence, there is no need for us to declare @v_name and @v_gender before using them.

After we call the stored procedure, MySQL will store the result of the SELECT statement (em_name and gender in this example) into the @v_name and @v_gender variables. We can then use these variables in subsequent SQL statements. For instance, if we run the previous CALL statement followed by the SELECT statement below:

```
SELECT * FROM employees WHERE gender = @v_gender;
```

we'll get the information of all male employees (since @v_gender = 'M' for employee 1).

Last but not least, let's look at an example of an INOUT parameter. Suppose we want to get the mentor_id of a record based on its mentee_id and project values, here's how we can do it:

```
DELIMITER $$

CREATE PROCEDURE get_mentor(INOUT p_em_id INT, IN
p_project VARCHAR(255))
BEGIN
    SELECT mentor_id INTO p_em_id FROM mentorships
WHERE mentee_id = p_em_id AND project = p_project;
END $$

DELIMITER ;
```

Here, p_em_id serves as both an IN and OUT parameter. Hence, we declare it as an INOUT parameter.

In order to call get_mentor(), we can first declare a variable called @v_id. Suppose we set it to 3 using the statement below:

```
SET @v_id = 3;
```

We can then pass this variable (@v_id) and the project name (e.g. 'Wayne Fibre') to the stored procedure as shown below:

```
CALL get_mentor(@v_id, 'Wayne Fibre');
```

When we do that, the stored procedure executes the SELECT statement within and updates the value of @v_id to 1 (which is the mentor_id returned by the SELECT statement). If we want to view the value of @v_id after the procedure is called, we use the following SELECT statement:

```
SELECT @v_id;
```

We'll get 1 as the output.

Stored Functions

Clear about stored procedures?

Great! Let's move on to stored functions. Stored functions are very similar to stored procedures except for some differences.

One of the key differences is that a stored function must return a value using the RETURN keyword. We'll learn how to do that later.

In addition, stored functions and stored procedures are executed differently. Stored functions are executed using a SELECT statement while stored procedures are executed using the CALL keyword.

We've already encountered some of the pre-written MySQL functions in Chapter 6.

Besides these pre-written functions provided by MySQL, we can write our own functions.

The basic syntax for writing a stored function in MySQL is:

```
DELIMITER $$

CREATE FUNCTION function_name([parameters, if any])
RETURNS data_type characteristics_of_function
BEGIN
   -- Details of function
RETURN result;
END $$

DELIMITER ;
```

The syntax may look confusing to you. Do not worry, let's look at an example to see how it works.

With reference to our **employees** table, suppose we want to calculate the amount of bonus to pay our employees. We can write a stored function to perform the calculation. The code below shows how it can be done:

```
DELIMITER $$

CREATE FUNCTION calculateBonus(p_salary DOUBLE,
p_multiple DOUBLE) RETURNS DOUBLE DETERMINISTIC
BEGIN
   DECLARE bonus DOUBLE(8, 2);
   SET bonus = p_salary*p_multiple;
   RETURN bonus;
END $$

DELIMITER ;
```

The name of the function is calculateBonus. It has two parameters - p_salary and p_multiple - both of DOUBLE type. You may notice that we did not specify whether these two parameters are IN, OUT or INOUT parameters. This is because stored functions can only have IN parameters. Hence, there is no need to use the IN keyword when declaring the parameters of a stored function.

After declaring the parameters, the two words RETURNS DOUBLE state that this function returns a result that is of DOUBLE type.

Next, we specify the characteristics of the function. Here, we state that the function is DETERMINISTIC.

DETERMINISTIC is a keyword that tells MySQL that the function will always return the same result given the same input parameters.

On the other hand, if we state that the function is NOT DETERMINISTIC, we are telling MySQL that the function may return a different result given the same input parameters.

Besides declaring a function as deterministic or otherwise, we can also state other characteristics of the function if we want.

These include NO SQL (indicates that the function does not contain SQL statements), READS SQL DATA (indicates that the function will only read data from the database, but will not modify the data), MODIFIES SQL DATA (indicates that the function may modify the data in the database) and CONTAINS SQL (indicates that the function contains SQL instructions, but does not contain statements that read or write data).

For instance, the following code states that demo_function is deterministic and contains SQL statements that modify SQL data:

```
CREATE FUNCTION demo_function(p_demo DOUBLE) RETURNS
DOUBLE DETERMINISTIC MODIFIES SQL DATA
```

Declaring the characteristics of a function is based on the "honestly" of the creator. The function will work even if it is declared wrongly. However, declaring a function wrongly may affect its results or performance.

After declaring the characteristics of our function, we proceed to the function definition enclosed between the BEGIN and END $$ markers.

The definition starts by declaring what is known as a local variable. A local variable is a special type of variable that is declared inside a stored routine and can only be used within the routine. To declare a local variable, we use the syntax below:

```
DECLARE name_of_variable data_type [DEFAULT
default_value];
```

In our example, we declared the variable as

```
DECLARE bonus DOUBLE(8, 2);
```

Here, the name of the variable is bonus and the data type is DOUBLE(8, 2).

We did not declare a default value for the variable. (Declaring a default value initializes the variable to that value. We'll see an example of that in Chapter 12.)

Instead, we set its value to p_salary*p_multiple using the SET keyword on the next line.

Finally, we return the value of bonus using the RETURN keyword:

```
RETURN bonus;
```

A function exits with a RETURN statement. Any task after the RETURN statement is ignored.

As you can see, the code for creating a stored function is very similar to that for creating a stored procedure, except for minor differences (like having to return a result). However, the way to call a stored function is very different. To call this function, we use it within a SELECT statement. For instance, we can do the following:

```
SELECT id, em_name, salary, calculateBonus(salary,
1.5) AS bonus FROM employees;
```

Here, we pass in the column `salary` and the value `1.5` to the `calculateBonus` function for the first and second parameters respectively. The fact that we did not prefix `salary` with @ indicates that `salary` is a column and not a user defined variable.

If we run the statement above, we'll get the following output.

id	em_name	salary	bonus
1	James Lee	3500	5250
2	Peter Pasternak	6010	9015
3	Clara Couto	3900	5850
6	Joyce Jones	8000	12000
7	Jason Cerrone	7980	11970
8	Prudence Phelps	11000	16500
9	Larry Zucker	3500	5250
11	Walker Welch	2500	3750

Deleting Stored Routines

Finally, before we end this chapter, let's talk about deleting stored routines.

While MySQL allows us to alter our stored routines (using the `ALTER` keyword), we can only make very limited modifications to it.

Hence, if we need to edit our stored routines, the easier way is actually to delete and recreate them.

To delete a stored procedure, we write

```
DROP PROCEDURE [IF EXISTS] name_of_procedure;
```

To delete a stored function, we write

```
DROP FUNCTION [IF EXISTS] name_of_function;
```

For instance, to delete the `calculateBonus` function, we write

```
DROP FUNCTION IF EXISTS calculateBonus;
```

Chapter 11: Control Flow Tools

Now that we know how to write basic stored routines, let us move on to a slightly more advanced concept.

In the previous chapter, we looked at a simple function for calculating the bonuses of employees. What if we want to perform more complex calculations?

For instance, suppose we want to pay 2 months bonus for employees with salary below 3000, but 1 month bonus for employees with salary above that?

In order to achieve the above, we need to use control flow tools. These include IF, CASE, and LOOP statements.

In this chapter, we'll be using a lot of examples to illustrate the concepts discussed. For each example, I'll leave a line before and after the control flow statements so that you can see clearly where they start and end.

Ready?

IF statement

Let's start with the IF statement. The syntax for the IF statement is as follows:

```
IF condition 1 is met THEN do task A;
   ELSEIF condition 2 is met THEN do task B;
   ELSEIF condition 3 is met THEN do task C;
   ...
   ELSE do task Z;
END IF;
```

The IF statement first checks if the first condition is met. If it is, it'll perform task A. If it is not, it'll move on to the first ELSEIF statement. If this condition is met, it'll perform task B. If it is not, it'll move down the ELSEIF statements until it finds a condition that is met. If no conditions are met, it'll perform task Z.

There can be as many ELSEIF statements as needed.

In addition, both the ELSEIF and ELSE statements are optional. You do not need to include them if there are no other conditions to check.

However, if you omit the ELSE statement and there exists a case that is not fulfilled by any of the IF and ELSEIF statements, MySQL will give you an error.

Let's look at some examples of the IF statement now.

Example 1

```
DELIMITER $$
CREATE FUNCTION if_demo_A(x INT) RETURNS VARCHAR(255)
DETERMINISTIC
BEGIN

   IF x > 0 THEN RETURN 'x is positive';
      ELSEIF x = 0 THEN RETURN 'x is zero';
      ELSE RETURN 'x is negative';
   END IF;

END $$
DELIMITER ;
```

This IF statement first checks if the input (x) is greater than zero. If it is, it returns 'x is positive'.

If it is not, it checks if x equals zero. If it is, it returns 'x is zero'.

If both the first two conditions are not met, it moves on to the `ELSE` statement and returns `'x is negative'`.

To run this function, we write

```
SELECT if_demo_A(2);
```

We'll get `'x is positive'`.

If we change the input from 2 to 0 or −1, we'll get `'x is zero'` and `'x is negative'` respectively.

Example 2

```
DELIMITER $$
CREATE FUNCTION if_demo_B(x INT) RETURNS VARCHAR(255)
DETERMINISTIC
BEGIN

    IF x > 0 THEN RETURN 'x is positive';
      ELSEIF x = 0 THEN RETURN 'x is zero';
    END IF;

END $$
DELIMITER ;
```

This example is similar to the previous one except that we omitted the `ELSE` statement. If we run the function now, we'll get the following outputs:

```
SELECT if_demo_B(2);
```

Output:
```
x is positive
```

```
SELECT if_demo_B(-1);
```

Output:

```
Error Code: 1321. FUNCTION if_demo_B ended without
RETURN
```

You can see that if we pass a value to the function that it is unable to process (a negative number in this case), the function returns an error.

CASE statement

Next, let's move on to CASE statements.

The CASE statement is very similar to the IF statement and can often be used interchangeably. In most cases, choosing between IF and CASE is a matter of personal preference.

The syntax is:

```
CASE case_variable
    WHEN value_1 THEN do task A;
    WHEN value_2 THEN do task B;
    . . .
    ELSE do task Z;
END CASE;
```

Or

```
CASE
    WHEN condition 1 is met THEN do task A;
    WHEN condition 2 is met THEN do task B;
    . . .
    ELSE do task Z;
END CASE;
```

The first syntax allows you to match the value of a variable against a set of distinct values. The second syntax allows you to perform more complex matches such as matching using ranges.

Let's look at some examples.

Example 1

```
DELIMITER $$
CREATE FUNCTION case_demo_A(x INT) RETURNS
VARCHAR(255) DETERMINISTIC
BEGIN

  CASE x
    WHEN 1 THEN RETURN 'x is 1';
    WHEN 2 THEN RETURN 'x is 2';
    ELSE RETURN 'x is neither 1 nor 2';
  END CASE;

END $$
DELIMITER ;
```

Calling the function:

```
SELECT case_demo_A(1);
```

Output:
```
x is 1
```

```
SELECT case_demo_A(5);
```

Output:
```
x is neither 1 nor 2
```

Example 2

```
DELIMITER $$
CREATE FUNCTION case_demo_B(x INT) RETURNS
VARCHAR(255) DETERMINISTIC
BEGIN

  CASE
    WHEN x > 0 THEN RETURN 'x is positive';
    WHEN x = 0 THEN RETURN 'x is zero';
```

```
        ELSE RETURN 'x is negative';
    END CASE;

END $$
DELIMITER ;
```

This second example uses the second syntax and tests x for a range instead of a single value.

Calling the function:

```
SELECT case_demo_B(1);
```

Output:
```
x is positive
```

```
SELECT case_demo_B(-1);
```

Output
```
x is negative
```

WHILE statement

The next control flow statement is the WHILE statement. This statement allows us to specify a task to be done repeatedly while a certain condition is valid.

The syntax is:

```
[name of while statement : ] WHILE condition is true
DO
   -- some tasks
END WHILE;
```

Example

```
DELIMITER $$
```

```
CREATE FUNCTION while_demo(x INT, y INT) RETURNS
VARCHAR(255) DETERMINISTIC
BEGIN
    DECLARE z VARCHAR(255);
    SET z = '';

    while_example: WHILE x<y DO
        SET x = x + 1;
        SET z = concat(z, x);
    END WHILE;

    RETURN z;
END $$
DELIMITER ;
```

Here, we first declare a local variable z and initialize it to an empty string (an empty string is a string with no content).

Next, we declare a WHILE statement. A WHILE statement can be labelled (but labelling it is optional). Here we label it while_example.

Next, the WHILE condition checks if x is smaller than y. (Both x and y are input parameters to the function.)

While x is smaller than y, the WHILE statement does the following:

First, it increases x by 1.
Next, it uses the concat() function to concatenate z with the new value of x.
Finally, it assigns the result back to z.

Recall that concat() is a built-in MySQL function that joins two strings together. If one (or both) of the values is a number (like in our example), it converts them to strings before joining them together.

After the WHILE statement, we simply return the value of z.

If you run the function using the following statement:

```
SELECT while_demo(1, 5);
```

you'll get
```
2345
```

as the output.

This is because when the loop starts, $x = 1$ and $y = 5$. As x is smaller than 5, the WHILE statement increases x by 1 ($x = 2$ now) and concatenates the result with z. Hence, $z = '2'$.

Next, the loop repeats itself. It increases x by 1 again ($x = 3$ now) and concatenates the result with z.

z becomes '23'.

These tasks of increasing x by 1 and concatenating the result with z are performed repetitively until the condition $x < y$ is no longer true.

REPEAT statement

Next, let's look at the REPEAT statement. A REPEAT statement is also used to perform repetitive tasks.

It repeatedly performs some tasks until the UNTIL condition <u>is met</u>. The syntax of a REPEAT statement is:

```
[name of repeat statement :] REPEAT
   -- do some tasks
   UNTIL stop condition is met
END REPEAT;
```

<u>Example</u>

```
DELIMITER $$
```

```
CREATE FUNCTION repeat_demo(x INT, y INT) RETURNS
VARCHAR(255) DETERMINISTIC
BEGIN
   DECLARE z VARCHAR(255);
   SET z = '';

   REPEAT
     SET x = x + 1;
     SET z = concat(z, x);
     UNTIL x>=y
   END REPEAT;

   RETURN z;
END $$
DELIMITER ;
```

This REPEAT statement repeats two tasks (SET x = x + 1 and SET z = concat(z, x)) until the x >= y condition is met.

If you run the function with the following statement

```
SELECT repeat_demo(1, 5);
```

You'll get the same output as the previous WHILE statement:
2345

As you can see, a REPEAT statement is very similar to a WHILE statement.

The main difference is that a REPEAT statement performs some tasks while a specified condition (in the UNTIL clause) is not met. On the other hand, a WHILE statement performs some tasks while a specified condition is met.

In addition, another important difference is that a REPEAT statement will always perform the tasks at least once. This is because the check (e.g. UNTIL x>=y) is done AFTER the tasks are completed.

Hence, if you run the following statement

```
SELECT repeat_demo(5, 1);
```

you'll get 6 as the result because even though the REPEAT condition (UNTIL x>=y) is already met, the two tasks inside the REPEAT statement are executed at least once since the check is done after the tasks are completed.

Clear?

LOOP statement

Last but not least, let's move on to the LOOP statement. This statement is very similar to the WHILE and REPEAT statements, except that it does not come with a condition to exit the loop.

Instead, we use the ITERATE or LEAVE keywords to exit it.

The syntax of a LOOP statement is:

```
[name of loop statement :] LOOP
   -- some tasks
END LOOP;
```

Let's look at a few examples.

Example 1

```
DELIMITER $$
CREATE FUNCTION loop_demo_A(x INT, y INT) RETURNS
VARCHAR(255) DETERMINISTIC
BEGIN
   DECLARE z VARCHAR(255);
   SET z = '';

   simple_loop: LOOP
```

```
    SET x = x + 1;
    IF x > y THEN
       LEAVE simple_loop;
    END IF;
    SET z = concat(z, x);
  END LOOP;

  RETURN z;
END $$
DELIMITER ;
```

Here, we declare a loop called simple_loop. Providing a name for a LOOP statement is often necessary as we need the name to use the LEAVE or ITERATE statements later.

Within the loop, we do the following:

First, we increase the value of x by 1.

Next, we check if x is greater than y. If it is, we leave the loop.

To leave the loop, we write

LEAVE simple_loop;

LEAVE is a keyword in MySQL to indicate that we want to exit the loop. We must provide the name of the loop to exit. In our example, we are exiting simple_loop.

If the LEAVE condition is not met, we remain in the loop and concatenate z with x.

If you run the function now with the following statement

```
SELECT loop_demo_A(1, 5);
```

you'll get
2345

as the output.

<u>Example 2</u>

Besides using the LEAVE keyword, we can also use the ITERATE keyword. In contrast to the LEAVE keyword that exits the loop completely, the ITERATE keyword only skips one iteration of the loop.

Let's look at an example:

```
DELIMITER $$
CREATE FUNCTION loop_demo_B(x INT, y INT) RETURNS
VARCHAR(255) DETERMINISTIC
BEGIN
   DECLARE z VARCHAR(255);
   SET z = '';

   simple_loop: LOOP
     SET x = x + 1;
     IF x = 3 THEN ITERATE simple_loop;
       ELSEIF x > y THEN LEAVE simple_loop;
     END IF;
     SET z = concat(z, x);
   END LOOP;

   RETURN z;
END $$
DELIMITER ;
```

Here, we added one more IF condition to our LOOP statement. This IF condition uses the ITERATE keyword.

If you run the function using the following statement,

```
SELECT loop_demo_B(1, 5);
```

you'll get

245

as the output.

The iteration $x = 3$ is skipped because of the condition

```
IF x = 3 THEN ITERATE simple_loop;
```

Clear?

Good!

With this example, we've come to the end of the chapter.

We'll be exploring one of the major uses of the LOOP statement in the next chapter.

Chapter 12: Cursors

Cool! We've come to the final chapter before the project.

In this chapter, we are going to look at a major use of the `LOOP` statement that we learned in the previous chapter.

Specifically, we'll be looking at cursors.

What is a Cursor?

First off, what is a cursor?

A cursor is a mechanism that allows us to step through the rows returned by a SQL statement.

So far, we have been learning to use `SELECT` statements to retrieve information from our tables. These statements return all the rows that match the stated criteria. However, there is no way for us to step through the rows one at a time.

If we want to do that, we have to use cursors.

The syntax for declaring a cursor is:

```
DECLARE cursor_name CURSOR FOR
    SELECT statement
```

This cursor declaration must be done after any variable declaration.

After declaring the cursor, we also need to declare a handler that defines what the cursor should do when it reaches the last row of the results returned by the `SELECT` statement. Normally, we want the cursor to set a variable to a certain value. For instance, we may want it to set a variable called `v_done` to `1`.

The syntax is:

```
DECLARE CONTINUE HANDLER FOR NOT FOUND SET
variable_name = value;
```

Next, we need to open the cursor using the statement:

```
OPEN cursor_name;
```

Once the cursor is open, we can use a loop to step through the rows. Within the loop, we need to retrieve the row that the cursor is currently pointing at and store the data into variables. The syntax for retrieving the row is:

```
FETCH cursor_name INTO variable_names;
```

After the row is retrieved, the cursor will automatically move to the next row. The LOOP statement will repeatedly fetch each row into the variables and process those variables until it reaches the end of the results.

When that happens, we leave the loop and close the cursor. The syntax for closing the cursor is:

```
CLOSE cursor_name;
```

Clear so far?

Example

Let's look at an example:

Suppose we want to get the names and genders of all employees in our **employees** table and combine them into a single line of text, here's how we do it:

```
DELIMITER $$
CREATE FUNCTION get_employees () RETURNS VARCHAR(255)
DETERMINISTIC
BEGIN
   DECLARE v_employees VARCHAR(255) DEFAULT '';
   DECLARE v_name VARCHAR(255);
   DECLARE v_gender CHAR(1);
   DECLARE v_done INT DEFAULT 0;

   DECLARE cur CURSOR FOR
      SELECT em_name, gender FROM employees;

   DECLARE CONTINUE HANDLER FOR NOT FOUND SET v_done =
1;

   OPEN cur;

   employees_loop: LOOP
      FETCH cur INTO v_name, v_gender;
      IF v_done = 1 THEN LEAVE employees_loop;
         ELSE SET v_employees = concat(v_employees, ',
', v_name, ': ', v_gender);
      END IF;
   END LOOP;

   CLOSE cur;

   RETURN substring(v_employees, 3);
END $$
DELIMITER ;
```

First, we declare a function called get_employees.

Within the function, we declare four local variables: v_employees,
v_name, v_gender and v_done and set the default values of
v_employees and v_done to ' ' and 0 respectively (using the
DEFAULT keyword).

Next, we declare a cursor called `cur` for the following `SELECT` statement:

```
SELECT em_name, gender FROM employees;
```

We also declare a handler called `v_done` for this cursor.

After that, we open the cursor and declare a loop called `employees_loop` to work with the cursor.

Within the loop, we fetch the row that `cur` is currently pointing at and store the results into the `v_name` and `v_gender` variables. We need to store the results into two variables as we selected two columns from the **employees** table.

Next, we check if `v_done` equals 1.

`v_done` equals 1 when the cursor reaches the end of the table (i.e. when there is no more data for the cursor to fetch).

If `v_done` equals 1, we exit the loop. Else, we use the `concat()` function to concatenate `v_employees` with `v_name` and `v_gender`, separated by a colon and comma.

The initial value of `v_employees` is an empty string (denoted by "). When we first concatenate `v_employees` with `', '`, `v_name`, `': '` and `v_gender`, we'll get

```
, James Lee: M
```

as `James Lee` and `M` is the name and gender of the first employee.

After we do this concatenation, we assign the concatenated result back to the `v_employees` variable.

The `LOOP` statement then repeats the same process for all the other rows in the table.

After looping, we close the cursor and return the value of `v_employees`. However, before we do that, we use the `substring()` function to remove the first comma from the string.

With that, the function is complete.

If you call this function using the statement

```
SELECT get_employees();
```

you'll get

```
James Lee: M, Peter Pasternak: M, Clara Couto: F,
Joyce Jones: F, Jason Cerrone: M, Prudence Phelps: F,
Larry Zucker: M, Walker Welch: M
```

as the result.

Chapter 13: Project

Great! We've covered all the fundamental concepts of MySQL. We are now ready to start working on our project. You are strongly encouraged to work through this project to help you gain a stronger grasp of the concepts covered.

The source code for the project can be downloaded at http://www.learncodingfast.com/sql.

Ready? Let's do it!

About the Project

This project requires us to build a simple database to help us manage the booking process of a sports complex. The sports complex has the following facilities: 2 tennis courts, 2 badminton courts, 2 multi-purpose fields and 1 archery range. Each facility can be booked for a duration of one hour.

Only registered users are allowed to make a booking. After booking, the complex allows users to cancel their bookings latest by the day prior to the booked date. Cancellation is free. However, if this is the third (or more) consecutive cancellations, the complex imposes a $10 fine.

The database that we build should have the following elements:

Tables

members
pending_terminations
rooms
bookings

View

member_bookings

Stored Procedures

insert_new_member
delete_member
update_member_password
update_member_email
make_booking
update_payment
view_bookings
search_room
cancel_booking

Trigger

payment_check

Stored Function

check_cancellation

We'll discuss the purpose of each as we go along.

Let's get started!

Creating the Database

The first thing that we need to do is create a database for our project.

Launch *MySQL Workbench* and create a new file by clicking on **File > New Query Tab**. Save this file as *sportsDB.sql* (**File > Save Script As...**).

We are going to create a database called `sports_booking`.

Enter the line

```
CREATE DATABASE sports_booking;
```

into *sportsDB.sql* and execute it.

If all goes well, you should see the message

```
1 row (s) affected
```

in the output window.

As we move forward with the project, you'll be asked to perform various SQL tasks. Do remember to click on the 'Execute Statement' button to **execute your SQL statements after each task**. This will allow you to check and correct any mistake as you go along.

In addition, you can also create another SQL file called *drop.sql*. If you make any mistake in your SQL code and need to make amendments, you can drop the object that you created using the *drop.sql* file.

For instance, if you named the database wrongly as `sports_bookingg`, you can add the following code to *drop.sql* to delete the database:

```
DROP DATABASE sports_bookingg;
```

After deleting, you can return to *sportsDB.sql* to recreate the database. Clear?

Let's move on.

Using the Database

Once you have created the `sports_booking` database, you need to tell MySQL that you want to use this database. Try doing that yourself (Hint: Refer to Chapter 2).

Adding Tables

Now, we are ready to add tables to our database. We need to add four tables: **members**, **pending_terminations**, **rooms** and **bookings**.

<u>members</u>

The **members** table has five columns:

`id`
This column stores the id of each member. The id is alphanumeric (`VARCHAR(255)` will be a good choice) and uniquely identifies each member (in other words, it is a primary key).

`password`
This column stores the password of each member. It is alphanumeric and cannot be null.

`email`
This column stores the email of each member. It is also alphanumeric and cannot be null.

`member_since`
This column stores the timestamp (consisting of the date and time) that a particular member is added to the table. It cannot be null and uses the `NOW()` function to get the current date and time as the `DEFAULT` value.

`payment_due`
This column stores the amount of balance that a member has to pay. The amount is in dollars and cents (e.g. 12.50). The column cannot be null and has a default value of 0.

Try creating this table yourself. You'll need to decide on the appropriate data type to use for each column and add the necessary restrictions (e.g. `NOT NULL`) yourself. You can refer to Chapter 3 for more information on creating tables.

Done?

The suggested code for this project can be found in Appendix C for reference if you run into any problems.

<u>pending_terminations</u>

Next, let's create the **pending_terminations** table. Records from the **members** table will be transferred here under certain circumstances.

The **pending_terminations** table has four columns: `id`, `email`, `request_date` and `payment_due`.

The data types and constraints of the `id`, `password` and `payment_due` columns match that of the same columns in the **members** table.

The remaining column, `request_date`, stores the timestamp that a particular member is added to the table. It cannot be null and uses the `NOW()` function to get the current date and time as the `DEFAULT` value.

Try creating this table yourself.

<u>rooms</u>

Now, let's move on to the **rooms** table. This table has three columns:

`id`
This column stores the id of each room. It is alphanumeric and uniquely identifies each room.

`room_type`
This column stores a short description of each room. It is also alphanumeric and cannot be null.

`price`
This column stores the price of each room. Prices are stored up to 2 decimal places. It cannot be null.

Try creating the **rooms** table.

Once you are done, we can move on to the hardest table - the **bookings** table.

bookings

The **bookings** table has 7 columns:

id
This column stores the id of each booking. It is numeric, auto incremented and uniquely identifies each booking.

room_id
This column has the same data type as the id column in the **rooms** table and cannot be null.

booked_date
This column stores a date in the YYYY-MM-DD format (e.g. '2017-10-18') and cannot be null.

booked_time
This column stores time in the HH:MM:SS format and cannot be null.

member_id
This column has the same data type as the id column in the **members** table and cannot be null.

datetime_of_booking
This column stores the timestamp that a particular booking is added to the table. It cannot be null and uses the NOW() function to get the current date and time as the DEFAULT value.

payment_status
This column stores the status of the booking. It is alphanumeric, cannot be null and has a default value of 'Unpaid'.

Besides the 7 columns stated above, the **bookings** table also has a `UNIQUE` constraint called `uc1`. This constraint states that the `room_id`, `booked_date` and `booked_time` columns must be unique. In other words, if one row has the values

```
room_id = 'AR', booked_date = '2017-10-18',
booked_time = '11:00:00'
```

no other rows can have the same combination of values for these three columns.

Try creating this table yourself.

Next, we need to alter our table to add two foreign keys:

The first foreign key is called `fk1` and links the `member_id` column with the `id` column in the **members** table. In addition, if the record in the parent table is updated or deleted, the record in the child table will also be updated or deleted accordingly.

The second foreign key is called `fk2` and links the `room_id` column with the `id` column in the **rooms** table. If the record in the parent table is updated or deleted, the record in the child table will also be updated or deleted accordingly.

Try updating the **bookings** table to add these two foreign keys.

Once you are done, our table creation is complete.

Inserting Data

Now, we need to add some values to our tables so that we have data to work with in the project later.

A PDF file containing data for these tables can be downloaded at
http://www.learncodingfast.com/sql. The tables can also be found in
Appendix B for easy reference.

members

For the **members** table, we have the following set of data:

id	password	email	member_since	payment_due
afeil	feil1988<3	Abdul.Feil@hotmail.com	2017-04-15 12:10:13	0.00
amely_18	loseweightin18	Amely.Bauch91@yahoo.com	2018-02-06 16:48:43	0.00
bbahringer	iambeau17	Beaulah_Bahringer@yahoo.com	2017-12-28 05:36:50	0.00
little31	whocares31	Anthony_Little31@gmail.com	2017-06-01 21:12:11	10.00
macejkovic73	jadajeda12	Jada.Macejkovic73@gmail.com	2017-05-30 17:30:22	0.00
marvin1	if0909mar	Marvin_Schulist@gmail.com	2017-09-09 02:30:49	10.00
nitzsche77	bret77@#	Bret_Nitzsche77@gmail.com	2018-01-09 17:36:49	0.00
noah51	18Oct1976#51	Noah51@gmail.com	2017-12-16 22:59:46	0.00
oreillys	reallycool#1	Martine_OReilly@yahoo.com	2017-10-12 05:39:20	0.00
wyattgreat	wyatt111	Wyatt_Wisozk2@gmail.com	2017-07-18 16:28:35	0.00

Try inserting these data yourself. For instance, for the first row, the code
would be

```
INSERT INTO members (id, password, email,
member_since, payment_due) VALUES
('afeil', 'feil1988<3', 'Abdul.Feil@hotmail.com',
'2017-04-15 12:10:13', 0);
```

Although member_since and payment_due both have default values,
we'll overwrite them here so that we have some variety in our data to
play with later. In addition, note that we enclosed the member_since
value in quotation marks. In general, we need to do that for TIMESTAMP,
DATETIME, DATE and TIME values.

Try modifying the code above to insert all the rows yourself.

Once you are done, you can move on to the **rooms** and **bookings**
tables.

rooms

id	room_type	price
AR	Archery Range	120.00
B1	Badminton Court	8.00
B2	Badminton Court	8.00
MPF1	Multi Purpose Field	50.00
MPF2	Multi Purpose Field	60.00
T1	Tennis Court	10.00
T2	Tennis Court	10.00

bookings

id	room_id	booked_date	booked_time	member_id	datetime_of_booking	payment_status
1	AR	2017-12-26	13:00:00	oreillys	2017-12-20 20:31:27	Paid
2	MPF1	2017-12-30	17:00:00	noah51	2017-12-22 05:22:10	Paid
3	T2	2017-12-31	16:00:00	macejkovic73	2017-12-28 18:14:23	Paid
4	T1	2018-03-05	08:00:00	little31	2018-02-22 20:19:17	Unpaid
5	MPF2	2018-03-02	11:00:00	marvin1	2018-03-01 16:13:45	Paid
6	B1	2018-03-28	16:00:00	marvin1	2018-03-23 22:46:36	Paid
7	B1	2018-04-15	14:00:00	macejkovic73	2018-04-12 22:23:20	Cancelled
8	T2	2018-04-23	13:00:00	macejkovic73	2018-04-19 10:49:00	Cancelled
9	T1	2018-05-25	10:00:00	marvin1	2018-05-21 11:20:46	Unpaid
10	B2	2018-06-12	15:00:00	bbahringer	2018-05-30 14:40:23	Paid

Try inserting data for these two tables yourself. These tables can be found in Appendix B for easy reference.

Done? Good!

View

Now that we have created the tables and inserted some data, we are ready to select data from our tables.

Specifically, we'll create a view that shows us all the booking details of a booking.

If you refer to the **bookings** table created previously, you can see that it lists the id, room_id, booked_date, booked_time, member_id, datetime_of_booking and payment_status of each booking.

What if in addition to the information above, we are also interested to know what each of the room ids stand for? For instance, we may want to know what AR stands for. In addition, what if we also want to know the price of each room?

In order to obtain these information, we have to refer to the **rooms** table.

To simplify this process, we are now going to write a SELECT statement to combine the two tables into a single view. This view displays the id (from the **bookings** table), room_id, room_type, booked_date, booked_time, member_id, datetime_of_booking, price and payment_status of each booking.

The room_type and price columns are from the **rooms** table while the remaining columns are from the **bookings** table.

In order to combine these two tables, we need a SELECT statement that joins the **rooms** and **bookings** tables. In addition, we also want to sort the results by the id column of the **bookings** table.

Try coding this statement yourself.

Hint: You need to join the two tables using bookings.room_id = rooms.id.

You can refer to Chapter 7 for reference on doing joins in SELECT statements.

Clear?

If you execute the SELECT statement, you should get the following table:

id	room_id	room_type	booked_date	booked_time	member_id	datetime_of_booking	price	payment_status
1	AR	Archery Range	2017-12-26	13:00:00	oreillys	2017-12-20 20:31:27	120.00	Paid
2	MPF1	Multi Purpose Field	2017-12-30	17:00:00	noah51	2017-12-22 05:22:10	50.00	Paid
3	T2	Tennis Court	2017-12-31	16:00:00	macejkovic73	2017-12-28 18:14:23	10.00	Paid
4	T1	Tennis Court	2018-03-05	08:00:00	little31	2018-02-22 20:19:17	10.00	Unpaid
5	MPF2	Multi Purpose Field	2018-03-02	11:00:00	marvin1	2018-03-01 16:13:45	60.00	Paid
6	B1	Badminton Court	2018-03-28	16:00:00	marvin1	2018-03-23 22:46:36	8.00	Paid
7	B1	Badminton Court	2018-04-15	14:00:00	macejkovic73	2018-04-12 22:23:20	8.00	Cancelled
8	T2	Tennis Court	2018-04-23	13:00:00	macejkovic73	2018-04-19 10:49:00	10.00	Cancelled
9	T1	Tennis Court	2018-05-25	10:00:00	marvin1	2018-05-21 11:20:46	10.00	Unpaid
10	B2	Badminton Court	2018-06-12	15:00:00	bbahringer	2018-05-30 14:40:23	8.00	Paid

Got it? Good!

Now, let's create a view for this SELECT statement. We'll call this view member_bookings. Try doing this yourself. You can refer to Chapter 8 for reference on creating views.

Once you are done, we can move on to create some stored procedures for our database.

Stored Procedures

In this exercise, we will create a total of nine stored procedures. Before we start coding them, let's first change the delimiter by adding the line

```
DELIMITER $$
```

to our *sportsDB.sql* file.

We'll code all the stored procedures after this line; there is no need to change the delimiter back to a semi-colon after each procedure. We'll change the delimiter back after we finish coding **all** the procedures and functions.

Ready?

insert_new_member

The first stored procedure is for inserting a new member into the **members** table.

If you study the structure of the **members** table, you can see that it has a total of 5 columns: `id`, `password`, `email`, `member_since` and `payment_due`.

As the last two columns have default values, we only need to provide values for the first three columns when inserting a new member.

To do that, let's create a stored procedure called `insert_new_member` that has three `IN` parameters, `p_id`, `p_password` and `p_email`. The data types for these parameters should match the data types that you selected for the `id`, `password` and `email` columns of the **members** table. Try declaring this stored procedure yourself. You can refer to Chapter 10 for reference.

Next, let's add the `BEGIN` and `END $$` markers to our stored procedure to define the start and end of this procedure.

Between the `BEGIN` and `END $$` markers, we need to add an `INSERT` statement to insert the values of `p_id`, `p_password` and `p_email` to our table. These values will be inserted into the `id`, `password` and `email` columns of the **members** table respectively.

A bit lost? Let's start with a hint for the first stored procedure.

Suppose we have a table called **demo_table** and we want to insert the value of a parameter called `p_age` to the `age` column of the table. Here's how we do it:

```
INSERT INTO demo_table (age) VALUES (p_age);
```

Try modifying the statement above and code the `insert_new_member` stored procedure yourself.

If you need help, you can refer to Chapter 4 and 10 for reference on writing an `INSERT` statement and a stored procedure respectively.

Once you have coded the stored procedure, you can place your cursor anywhere between the BEGIN and END $$ markers and click on the 'Execute Statement' button to execute this procedure. (Remember to do so for all subsequent stored procedures and functions.)

If all goes well, you should get a green tick in the output window.

The suggested solution is provided in Appendix C and can be downloaded from http://www.learncodingfast.com/sql.

delete_member

Next, let's move on to the delete_member procedure. As the name suggests, this procedure is for deleting a member from the **members** table.

This stored procedure only has one IN parameter, p_id. Its data type matches that of the id column in the **members** table.

Within the procedure, we have a DELETE statement that deletes the member whose id equals p_id. Try coding this procedure yourself.

update_member_password and update_member_email

Next, we'll code two stored procedures to help us update data in the **members** table.

The first stored procedure is called update_member_password and has two IN parameters, p_id and p_password.

The second procedure is called update_member_email and has two IN parameters, p_id and p_email.

The data types of all parameters match the data types of the corresponding columns in the **members** table.

Both procedures use the UPDATE statement to update the password and email of a member with id = p_id. Try coding them yourself.

Once you are done, we can move on to the `make_booking` procedure.

make_booking

The `make_booking` procedure is for making a new booking. We need to insert the booking into the **bookings** table and update the **members** table to reflect the charges that the member making the booking needs to pay.

The procedure has four `IN` parameters, `p_room_id`, `p_booked_date`, `p_booked_time` and `p_member_id`.

The data types of the parameters match the data types of the `room_id`, `booked_date`, `booked_time` and `member_id` columns of the **bookings** table.

Within the procedure, we first declare two local variables `v_price` and `v_payment_due`. The data type of `v_price` matches the data type of the `price` column in the **rooms** table while that of `v_payment_due` matches the data type of the `payment_due` column in the **members** table.

Try declaring these variables yourself. Refer to Chapter 10 (under Stored Functions) if you have forgotten how to declare a local variable.

After declaring the variables, we have the following `SELECT` statement:

```
SELECT price INTO v_price FROM rooms WHERE id =
p_room_id;
```

This statement selects the price of the room with `id = p_room_id`. This price is then stored into the local variable `v_price` using the `INTO` keyword.

Next, we need an `INSERT` statement to insert the values of `p_room_id`, `p_booked_date`, `p_booked_time` and `p_member_id` into the room_id, booked_date, booked_time and member_id columns of the **bookings** table respectively.

Try coding this INSERT statement yourself.

After updating the **bookings** table, we need to update the payment_due column of the **members** table.

To do that, we need to first get the payment_due value for the member making the booking. We get that from the **members** table (WHERE id = p_member_id) and store the information into the v_payment_due variable.

Next, we update the **members** table and set the payment_due column to v_payment_due + v_price for this particular member (WHERE id = p_member_id).

Try writing the SELECT and UPDATE statements yourself.

Once that is done, the make_booking procedure is complete.

update_payment

Now, let's move on to the update_payment procedure.

This procedure is for updating the **bookings** and **members** tables after a member makes payment for his/her booking.

By default, the payment_status column in the **bookings** table is 'Unpaid'. Once the member makes payment, this status will be updated to 'Paid'.

After updating the **bookings** table, the **members** table will also be updated to reflect the new amount of money (if any) the member has to pay.

The `update_payment` procedure has one `IN` parameter called `p_id`, whose data type matches the `id` column of the **bookings** table.

Within the procedure, we need to first declare three local variables, `v_member_id`, `v_payment_due` and `v_price`.

The data types of `v_member_id` and `v_payment_due` match the data types of the `id` and `payment_due` columns in the **members** table while the data type of `v_price` matches the data type of the `price` column in the **rooms** table.

Try declaring these variables yourself.

Next, we need to use an `UPDATE` statement to update the **bookings** table. Specifically, we need to change the `payment_status` of the specified booking (whose `id` corresponds to the input parameter `p_id`) to `'Paid'`.

Try doing it yourself.

After updating the **bookings** table, we need to update the `payment_due` column of the **members** table for the member who made the booking.

To do that, we need to first select the `member_id` and `price` columns from the `member_bookings` <u>view</u> for this particular booking (`WHERE id = p_id`) and store the information into the `v_member_id` and `v_price` variables respectively.

In addition, we need to select the `payment_due` column from the **members** table for the member who made the booking and store the information into the `v_payment_due` variable. Note that the local variable `v_member_id` stores the `id` of the member who made the booking.

Try coding these two `SELECT` statements yourself.

After gathering the information that we need, we are now ready to update the **members** table. We'll use the UPDATE statement to set the payment_due column to v_payment_due - v_price for the member who made the booking (WHERE id = v_member_id).

Try coding this UPDATE statement yourself. Once that is done, the procedure is complete.

view_bookings

Next, let's move on to the view_bookings procedure.

This procedure allows us to view all the bookings made by a particular member and has one IN parameter called p_id that identifies the member. Decide on the appropriate data type for this parameter and declare the procedure yourself.

Within the procedure, we have a simple SELECT statement that selects everything from the member_bookings view for that particular member.

Try doing it yourself.

search_room

Now, let's move on to the seach_room procedure. This procedure allows us to search for available rooms.

It has three IN parameters, p_room_type, p_booked_date and p_booked_time. Choose an appropriate data type for each parameter based on the room_type column in the **rooms** table (for p_room_type) and the booked_date and booked_time columns in **bookings** table (for p_booked_date and p_booked_time respectively).

Within the procedure, we have a single SELECT statement to check if a certain room is available for booking on a specific date and time. Let's work on this SELECT statement now.

As this statement is relatively complex, let us work on a separate SQL file first. Create a new SQL file in *MySQL Workbench* and save it as *trial.sql*.

Now, in *trial.sql*, try writing a SELECT statement to select all the information from the **bookings** table and execute that statement.

Done? Good.

Now, let's do some filtering. Suppose we are only interested in bookings where

```
booked_date = '2017-12-26' AND booked_time =
'13:00:00' AND payment_status != 'Cancelled'
```

Try to modify your SELECT statement such that it only shows these rooms.

You should get the following result:

id	room_id	booked_date	booked_time	memb...	datetime_of_booking	payment_...
1	AR	2017-12-26	13:00:00	oreillys	2017-12-20 20:31:27	Paid

Finally, modify the statement such that only the room_id column is displayed.

If you execute the statement, you should just get AR as the result.

Got it? Now we have the ids of <u>all the rooms that have been booked on 2017-12-26 at 1pm and have not been cancelled</u>.

Suppose we want to book a tennis court on 2017-12-26 at 1pm, all we need to do is select rooms from the **rooms** table whose ids are <u>not</u> in the results above AND are of the room type that we want (i.e. room_type = 'Tennis Court').

Try to write a SELECT statement to achieve that. (Hint: You need to use the previous SELECT statement as a subquery.)

Manage to do it? You should get the following results:

id	room_type	price
T1	Tennis Court	10.00
T2	Tennis Court	10.00

Once you get the correct result, you are ready to get back to the search_room stored procedure.

For this stored procedure, you simply need to paste the previous SELECT statement into the procedure (between the BEGIN and END $$ markers) and change

'Tennis Court' to p_room_type,
'2017-12-26' to p_booked_date, and
'13:00:00' to p_booked_time.

With that, the stored procedure is complete. You can refer to the suggested solution in Appendix C if you are stuck.

Once you are done, we can move on to the most complicated procedure.

cancel_booking

This last procedure is for making a booking cancellation. This procedure requires the use of an IF statement.

First, let's name the procedure cancel_booking. This procedure has an IN parameter called p_booking_id (whose data type corresponds to the data type of the id column in the **bookings** table) and an OUT parameter called p_message (that is of VARCHAR(255) type).

Within the procedure, we need to declare 6 local variables - v_cancellation, v_member_id, v_payment_status, v_booked_date, v_price and v_payment_due.

The data type of v_cancellation is INT while those of v_member_id, v_payment_status and v_booked_date match the data types of the member_id, payment_status and booked_date columns in the **bookings** table respectively.

In addition, the data type of v_price matches the data type of the price column in the **rooms** table and the data type of v_payment_due matches the data type of the payment_due column in the **members** table.

Try declaring the variables yourself.

Next, let's set the value of v_cancellation to 0 using the SET keyword.

Done?

Now, we need to select the member_id, booked_date, price and payment_status columns from the member_bookings view where id = p_booking_id and store them into the v_member_id, v_booked_date, v_price and v_payment_status variables respectively.

In addition, we need to select the payment_due column from the **members** table for the member making the cancellation (WHERE id = v_member_id) and store the result into the v_payment_due variable.

Try doing these yourself.

Once you are done, we are ready to work on the IF statement.

The sports complex allows members to cancel their bookings latest by the day prior to the booked date.

For instance, if the booked date is 17th Sep 2018 and the current date is 16th Sep 2018, members will be allowed to cancel their booking. However, if the current date is 17th Sep 2018 or later, members will not be allowed to cancel the booking.

In addition, members are not allowed to cancel bookings that have already been cancelled or paid for.

To enforce these rules, we'll use the following IF statement:

```
IF curdate() >= v_booked_date THEN
   SELECT 'Cancellation cannot be done on/after the
booked date'  INTO p_message;
   ELSEIF v_payment_status = 'Cancelled' OR
v_payment_status = 'Paid' THEN
      SELECT 'Booking has already been cancelled or
paid'  INTO p_message;
   ELSE
      -- Code to handle cancellation
END IF;
```

Let's analyze this IF statement.

In the IF clause, we first use the built-in CURDATE() function to get the current date.

If the current date is greater than or equal to the booked date, we use a SELECT statement to store the message

```
'Cancellation cannot be done on/after the booked
date'
```

into the OUT parameter p_message.

Next, we proceed to the ELSEIF clause. Here, we use the v_payment_status variable to check if the booking has already been cancelled or paid for. If it has, we store the message

`'Booking has already been cancelled or paid'`

into the `OUT` parameter.

Finally, we proceed to the `ELSE` clause. This is where we handle the actual cancellation.

Clear? Good!

Now that we are clear about the `IF` statement, let's work on the cancellation code for the `ELSE` clause. You can replace the comment

`-- Code to handle cancellation`

with code that we'll be writing next.

To handle the cancellation, we need to do a couple of steps:

First, we need to update the **bookings** table to change the `payment_status` column to `'Cancelled'` for this particular booking.

Next, we need to calculate the new amount that the member who made this booking has to pay and update the `payment_due` column for this member in the **members** table.

Finally, we need to store the message `'Booking Cancelled'` into the `OUT` parameter to indicate that the booking has been cancelled.

Step 1

To update the **bookings** table, we simply need to write an `UPDATE` statement to change the `payment_status` column to `'Cancelled'` for this particular booking (`WHERE id = p_booking_id`).

Try doing this yourself.

Step 2

Next, we need to calculate how much the member owes the sports complex now.

As the booking has been cancelled, the member no longer needs to pay for the booking. Hence, we need to first set the value of `v_payment_due` to `v_payment_due - v_price` using a `SET` statement.

Try doing this yourself.

Next, we need to check if this is the third consecutive cancellation by the member. If it is, we'll impose a $10 fine on the member.

To do that, we'll use a function called `check_cancellation`. We'll code this function later. For now, we simply need to use the function in our stored procedure.

This function takes in one value - the booking id.

Try calling the function, passing in the booking id (`p_booking_id`) and assigning the result of the function to the local variable `v_cancellation`. (Recall: You need to use the `SET` keyword to assign the result of the function to the variable.)

Done?

Next, we need another `IF` statement. This <u>inner `IF`</u> statement checks if `v_cancellation` is greater than or equal to 2. If it is, we have to add 10 to `v_payment_due` and assign it back to `v_payment_due`.

Try coding the `IF` statement yourself.

`v_payment_due` now stores the final updated amount that the member has to pay the complex.

Now, we simply need to use an UPDATE statement to update the value of payment_due in the **members** table for this particular member (WHERE id = v_member_id).

Clear? Try doing this yourself.

<u>Step 3</u>

For the last step, we simply need to use a SELECT statement to store the message 'Booking Cancelled' into the OUT parameter.

Try doing it yourself. Once you are done, the ELSE clause is complete and so is the stored procedure.

Trigger

Now that we have finished coding our stored procedures, let's move on to triggers. We'll only be coding one trigger - payment_check.

This trigger checks the outstanding balance of a member, which is recorded in the payment_due column of the **members** table.

If payment_due is more than $0 and the member terminates his/her account, we'll transfer the data to the **pending_terminations** table. This table records all the termination requests that are pending due to an outstanding payment.

Let's first declare the trigger as follows:

```
CREATE TRIGGER payment_check BEFORE DELETE ON members
FOR EACH ROW
```

As you can see, this trigger is activated when we try to delete a record from the **members** table.

Next, between the BEGIN and END $$ markers, we need to do a few things:

First, we need to declare a local variable called v_payment_due. The data type of v_payment_due matches that of the payment_due column in the **members** table.

Next, we need to select the payment_due column from the **members** table for the member that we are trying to delete and store that data into the v_payment_due variable. (Hint: As this trigger is activated by a DELETE event, we need to use OLD.id to retrieve his/her id.)

After getting the v_payment_due value, we'll use an IF statement to check if v_payment_due is greater than 0.

If it is, we'll use an INSERT statement to insert a new record into the **pending_terminations** table. This new record contains the id, email and payment_due values of the member that we are trying to delete.

Once that is done, the trigger is complete.

Try coding this trigger yourself. You can refer to Chapter 9 for reference if you have forgotten how to code a trigger.

Stored Function

The final thing that we need to code is the check_cancellation function.

This function checks the number of consecutive cancellations made by the member who's trying to cancel a booking. It has one parameter p_booking_id whose data type matches that of the id column in the **bookings** table. In addition, it returns an integer and is deterministic.

Try declaring this function yourself. You can refer to Chapter 10 for reference on declaring a function.

Within the function (between the BEGIN and END $$ markers), we need to use a cursor to loop through the **bookings** table vertically. To begin, let's first declare three local variables called v_done, v_cancellation and v_current_payment_status.

Both v_done and v_cancellation are of INT type.

v_current_payment_status, on the other hand, has a data type that matches the data type of the payment_status column in the **bookings** table.

Next, we need to use a SELECT statement to select the payment_status column (from the **bookings** table) of the member who's trying to do a cancellation.

This is a relatively complex statement, so we'll do it in *trial.sql* first.

Suppose we are trying to do a cancellation of the booking with id = 5. We need to first get the member_id of the member who made this booking. Try writing a SELECT statement to get the member_id from the **bookings** table.

Next, using this member_id, we need to get the payment_status of all the bookings made by this member.

To do that, you need to select the payment_status column from the **bookings** table, using the previous SELECT statement as a subquery. Try doing it yourself.

Finally, we need to order the results by datetime_of_booking in descending order so that we get the latest payment_status first.

Got it?

Once you are done, execute the statement. You should get the following results:

```
Unpaid
Paid
Paid
```

With that, you can return to the *sportsDB.sql* fie and continue working on the `check_cancellation` function.

Copy and paste the query you just wrote into the function and change the `WHERE` clause in the subquery from

```
WHERE id = 5
```

to

```
WHERE id = p_booking_id
```

We need to declare a cursor for this `SELECT` statement.

Let's name this cursor `cur` and try declaring it yourself. You can refer to Chapter 12 if you need help on declaring a cursor.

Done?

Once you have declared the cursor, you need to declare a `CONTINUE HANDLER` for this cursor. This can be done using the statement below:

```
DECLARE CONTINUE HANDLER FOR NOT FOUND SET v_done =
1;
```

So far so good?

Great! Let's move on.

Now, we need to set the values of `v_done` and `v_cancellation` to `0` using the `SET` keyword.

Try doing it yourself.

Once we have declared and set everything that we need, we are ready to start looping through the `payment_status` column.

We need to do the following 4 things:
1. Open the cursor
2. Use the cursor to loop through the `payment_status` column and increment `v_cancellation` by 1 for each consecutive cancellation
3. Close the cursor
4. Return the value of `v_cancellation`

Step 1 should be quite straightforward. Try doing it yourself.

Next, we need to work on the loop for the cursor.

Let's call this loop `cancellation_loop`.

Within the loop, we need to use the `FETCH` statement to fetch the value that the cursor is currently pointing at into the `v_current_payment_status` variable.

Try doing this yourself.

After fetching the value, we'll use an `IF` statement to check the values of `v_current_payment_status` and `v_done`.

If `v_current_payment_status` does not equal `'Cancelled'` or `v_done` equals `1`, we can leave the loop. This is because once we find a `v_current_payment_status` that is not equal to `'Cancelled'`, the string of consecutive cancellations (if any) has ended.

In addition, if `v_done` equals `1`, we have come to the end of the result set from the `SELECT` statement and can also leave the loop.

Clear? Try coding the `IF` clause yourself.

Once you are done with the `IF` clause, you can work on the `ELSE` clause.

Within the `ELSE` clause, we simply increment the value of `v_cancellation` by 1 using the `SET` keyword.

Try coding this `ELSE` clause yourself.

Once you are done, you can end the `IF` statement, end the loop, close the cursor and return the value of `v_cancellation`. Try doing these yourself.

Chapter 12 provides an example on coding a similar loop. Do check it out if you are stuck.

Once that is complete, we have finished coding our stored routines. We can now change the delimiter back to a semi-colon using the statement below:

```
DELIMITER ;
```

With that, we have come to the end of our project coding.

Congratulations!

We are now ready to try out some of its features.

Excited? Let's do it!

Testing the Database

To test our database, let's create a new SQL file called *test.sql*. We'll do all our testing on this file.

First, we'll check if our tables are created correctly. Try executing the following statements to check if the tables are correct:

```
SELECT * FROM members;
SELECT * FROM pending_terminations;
SELECT * FROM bookings;
SELECT * FROM rooms;
```

members, **bookings** and **rooms** should contain the same information as the respective tables shown in Appendix B.

pending_terminations, on the other hand, should be empty.

Got it? Good!

Next, let's try the `insert_new_member` procedure. Try executing the following statements:

```
CALL insert_new_member ('angelolott', '1234abcd',
'AngeloNLott@gmail.com');

SELECT * FROM members ORDER BY member_since DESC;
```

You should get the table below. The new member added is shown on the first row of the table.

id	password	email	member_since	payment_due
angelolott	1234abcd	AngeloNLott@gmail.com	2018-10-10 21:28:34	0.00
amely_18	loseweightin18	Amely.Bauch91@yahoo....	2018-02-06 16:48:43	0.00
nitzsche77	bret77@#	Bret_Nitzsche77@gmail....	2018-01-09 17:36:49	0.00
bbahringer	iambeau17	Beaulah_Bahringer@yah...	2017-12-28 05:36:50	0.00
noah51	18Oct1976#51	Noah51@gmail.com	2017-12-16 22:59:46	0.00
oreillys	reallycool#1	Martine_OReilly@yahoo....	2017-10-12 05:39:20	0.00
marvin1	if0909mar	Marvin_Schulist@gmail....	2017-09-09 02:30:49	10.00
wyattgreat	wyatt111	Wyatt_Wisozk2@gmail.c...	2017-07-18 16:28:35	0.00
little31	whocares31	Anthony_Little31@gmail...	2017-06-01 21:12:11	10.00
macejkovic73	jadajeda12	Jada.Macejkovic73@gm...	2017-05-30 17:30:22	0.00
afeil	feil1988<3	Abdul.Feil@hotmail.com	2017-04-15 12:10:13	0.00

Got it?

Now we'll delete two members from this table. The two members that we'll delete are `little31` and `afeil`. Note that `little31` has an outstanding payment of $10.

Try executing the following statements:

```
CALL delete_member ('afeil');
CALL delete_member ('little31');
SELECT * FROM members;
SELECT * FROM pending_terminations;
```

You should see that both `afeil` and `little31` are deleted from the **members** table. However, as `little31` has an outstanding payment of $10, a new record is added to the **pending_terminations** table. This is due to the `payment_check` trigger that we wrote.

Got it? Cool!

Next, let's try updating a member's password and email. Try executing the following statements:

```
CALL update_member_password ('noah51', '18Oct1976');
CALL update_member_email ('noah51',
'noah51@hotmail.com');
SELECT * FROM members;
```

You should see the password and email address of `noah51` updated to `18Oct1976` and `noah51@hotmail.com` respectively.

Next, we'll test the `update_payment` procedure. Before we do that, let's first run the following two statements:

```
SELECT * FROM members WHERE id = 'marvin1';
SELECT * FROM bookings WHERE member_id = 'marvin1';
```

You should see that `marvin1` has an outstanding payment of `10.00` in the **members** table and an unpaid booking (`id = 9`) in the **bookings** table.

We'll update the payment status (from `'Paid'` to `'UnPaid'`) for this booking.

Try executing the following statements:

```
CALL update_payment (9);
SELECT * FROM members WHERE id = 'marvin1';
SELECT * FROM bookings WHERE member_id = 'marvin1';
```

The `payment_due` column for `marvin1` in the **members** table should now show `0.00` and the `payment_status` column in the **bookings** table should be updated to `Paid`.

Next, let's try the `search_room` procedure. Try executing the following statement:

```
CALL search_room('Archery Range', '2017-12-26',
'13:00:00');
```

You should see no results in the "Result Grid".

This is because the "Archery Range" room is already booked on 2017-12-26 at 1pm.

Next, try executing

```
CALL search_room('Badminton Court', '2018-04-15',
'14:00:00');
```

You should get two rows returned as both badminton courts (`B1` and `B2`) are available on 2018-04-15 at 2pm.

Note that `B1` has previously been booked by `macejkovic73` (`id = 7` in the **bookings** table).

However, the booking was eventually cancelled. Hence, it shows up as available when we do a search.

Finally, try executing

```
CALL search_room('Badminton Court', '2018-06-12',
'15:00:00');
```

You should only get one row returned (B1). This is because B2 has already been booked for the specified date and time (id = 10 in the **bookings** table).

Next, let's try to make a booking. Try executing the following statement:

```
CALL make_booking ('AR', '2017-12-26', '13:00:00',
'noah51');
```

You should get the following error message:

```
Error Code: 1062. Duplicate entry 'AR-2017-12-26-
13:00:00' for key 'uc1'
```

This is due to the unique key constraint (uc1) that we added to the **bookings** table.

As we already have a row with room_id = 'AR', booked_date = '2017-12-26' and booked_time = '13:00:00' (id = 1 in the **bookings** table), we are not allowed to add another entry with the same values.

Next, try executing the following statements:

```
CALL make_booking ('T1', CURDATE() + INTERVAL 2 WEEK,
'11:00:00', 'noah51');
CALL make_booking ('AR', CURDATE() + INTERVAL 2 WEEK,
'11:00:00', 'macejkovic73');
SELECT * FROM bookings;
```

You should see two new bookings added to the **bookings** table. Take note of the booking ids for these bookings. We'll need them later.

If you study the code above, you may notice something new. For the two CALL statements, instead of providing the make_booking procedure with a date (such as '2017-12-26'), we provided it with

```
CURDATE() + INTERVAL 2 WEEK
```

Here, we use the built-in CURDATE() function to get the current date. Next, we use the INTERVAL keyword to add an interval of 2 weeks to the current date.

The INTERVAL keyword can be used to add or subtract intervals (such as 1 DAY, 2 MONTH etc) from a specified date.

The code above allows us to make bookings two weeks from the current date. For instance, if the current date is 1st Oct, the bookings will be for 15th Oct.

Clear? Great! Let's move on to test the final procedure - cancel_booking.

Try executing the following statements:

```
CALL cancel_booking(1, @message);
SELECT @message;
```

You should get the message

```
Cancellation cannot be done on/after the booked date
```

in the "Result Grid". This is because the booked date for booking 1 is 2017-12-26, which is already over.

Next, replace *** in the statement below with the booking id of the new booking made by noah51 and execute the two statements:

```
CALL cancel_booking(***, @message);
SELECT @message;
```

You should get the message

```
Booking Cancelled
```

indicating that the cancellation is successful.

Finally, execute the following statements, replacing ^^^ with the booking id of the new booking made by macejkovic73:

```
CALL cancel_booking(^^^, @message);
SELECT @message;
```

You should also get the message

```
Booking Cancelled
```

However, if you execute the following statement now

```
SELECT * FROM members;
```

You should notice that the payment_due value of noah51 is 0 while that of macejkovic73 is 10.

macejkovic73 has a payment_due of $10 because the most recent cancellation is the 3rd consecutive cancellation. Hence, a $10 fine is imposed. This is due to the

```
IF v_cancellation >= 2 THEN
   SET v_payment_due = v_payment_due + 10;
END IF;
```

code that we wrote in the cancel_booking procedure.

Clear?

With this, we've come to the end of the book!

Congratulations and give yourself a pat on the shoulder!

I sincerely hope you've found this book useful and that you've enjoyed the course.

If you run into any problems with the project, do not be discouraged. I strongly encourage you to download the source code from http://www.learncodingfast.com/sql and compare your code with the suggested solution. Finding errors and amending your code is one of the best way to learn.

Have fun learning and thank you once again!

Appendix A: Tables for companyHR

employees

id	em_name	gender	contact_number	salary	years_in_co...	date_created
1	James Lee	M	516-514-1729	3500	11	2007-09-21 11:20:46
2	Peter Pasternak	M	845-644-7919	6010	10	2008-09-12 22:23:20
3	Clara Couto	F	845-641-5236	3900	8	2010-11-01 16:13:45
6	Joyce Jones	F	523-172-2191	8000	3	2015-06-22 12:21:46
7	Jason Cerrone	M	725-441-7172	7980	2	2016-01-25 15:22:16
8	Prudence Phelps	F	546-312-5112	11000	2	2016-09-12 12:20:22
9	Larry Zucker	M	817-267-9799	3500	1	2017-03-12 11:18:16
10	Serena Parker	F	621-211-7342	12000	1	2017-10-18 18:14:23
11	Walker Welch	M	NULL	2500	4	2014-10-30 13:41:23

mentorships

mentor_id	mentee_id	status	project
1	2	Ongoing	SQF Limited
1	3	Past	Wayne Fibre
2	3	Ongoing	SQF Limited
3	11	Ongoing	SQF Limited

Appendix B: Tables for sportsDB

members

id	password	email	member_since	payment_due
afeil	feil1988<3	Abdul.Feil@hotmail.com	2017-04-15 12:10:13	0.00
amely_18	loseweightin18	Amely.Bauch91@yahoo.com	2018-02-06 16:48:43	0.00
bbahringer	iambeau17	Beaulah_Bahringer@yahoo.com	2017-12-28 05:36:50	0.00
little31	whocares31	Anthony_Little31@gmail.com	2017-06-01 21:12:11	10.00
macejkovic73	jadajeda12	Jada.Macejkovic73@gmail.com	2017-05-30 17:30:22	0.00
marvin1	if0909mar	Marvin_Schulist@gmail.com	2017-09-09 02:30:49	10.00
nitzsche77	bret77@#	Bret_Nitzsche77@gmail.com	2018-01-09 17:36:49	0.00
noah51	18Oct1976#51	Noah51@gmail.com	2017-12-16 22:59:46	0.00
oreillys	reallycool#1	Martine_OReilly@yahoo.com	2017-10-12 05:39:20	0.00
wyattgreat	wyatt111	Wyatt_Wisozk2@gmail.com	2017-07-18 16:28:35	0.00

bookings

id	room_id	booked_date	booked_time	member_id	datetime_of_booking	payment_status
1	AR	2017-12-26	13:00:00	oreillys	2017-12-20 20:31:27	Paid
2	MPF1	2017-12-30	17:00:00	noah51	2017-12-22 05:22:10	Paid
3	T2	2017-12-31	16:00:00	macejkovic73	2017-12-28 18:14:23	Paid
4	T1	2018-03-05	08:00:00	little31	2018-02-22 20:19:17	Unpaid
5	MPF2	2018-03-02	11:00:00	marvin1	2018-03-01 16:13:45	Paid
6	B1	2018-03-28	16:00:00	marvin1	2018-03-23 22:46:36	Paid
7	B1	2018-04-15	14:00:00	macejkovic73	2018-04-12 22:23:20	Cancelled
8	T2	2018-04-23	13:00:00	macejkovic73	2018-04-19 10:49:00	Cancelled
9	T1	2018-05-25	10:00:00	marvin1	2018-05-21 11:20:46	Unpaid
10	B2	2018-06-12	15:00:00	bbahringer	2018-05-30 14:40:23	Paid

rooms

id	room_type	price
AR	Archery Range	120.00
B1	Badminton Court	8.00
B2	Badminton Court	8.00
MPF1	Multi Purpose Field	50.00
MPF2	Multi Purpose Field	60.00
T1	Tennis Court	10.00
T2	Tennis Court	10.00

Appendix C: Suggested Solution for Project

sportsDB.sql

```sql
CREATE DATABASE sports_booking;
USE sports_booking;

-- ************* CREATE TABLES *************

CREATE TABLE members (
    id VARCHAR(255) PRIMARY KEY,
    password VARCHAR(255) NOT NULL,
    email VARCHAR(255) NOT NULL,
    member_since TIMESTAMP DEFAULT NOW() NOT NULL,
    payment_due DECIMAL(6, 2) NOT NULL DEFAULT 0
);

CREATE TABLE pending_terminations (
    id VARCHAR(255) PRIMARY KEY,
    email VARCHAR(255) NOT NULL,
    request_date TIMESTAMP DEFAULT NOW() NOT NULL,
    payment_due DECIMAL(6, 2) NOT NULL DEFAULT 0
);

CREATE TABLE rooms (
    id VARCHAR(255) PRIMARY KEY,
    room_type VARCHAR(255) NOT NULL,
    price DECIMAL(6, 2) NOT NULL
);

CREATE TABLE bookings (
    id INT AUTO_INCREMENT PRIMARY KEY,
    room_id VARCHAR(255) NOT NULL,
    booked_date DATE NOT NULL,
    booked_time TIME NOT NULL,
    member_id VARCHAR(255) NOT NULL,
    datetime_of_booking TIMESTAMP DEFAULT NOW() NOT NULL,
    payment_status VARCHAR(255) NOT NULL DEFAULT 'Unpaid',
    CONSTRAINT uc1 UNIQUE (room_id, booked_date, booked_time)
```

```sql
);

ALTER TABLE bookings
    ADD CONSTRAINT fk1 FOREIGN KEY (member_id) REFERENCES
members (id) ON DELETE CASCADE ON UPDATE CASCADE,
    ADD CONSTRAINT fk2 FOREIGN KEY (room_id) REFERENCES rooms
(id) ON DELETE CASCADE ON UPDATE CASCADE;

-- ************* INSERT DATA *************

INSERT INTO members (id, password, email, member_since,
payment_due) VALUES
('afeil', 'feil1988<3', 'Abdul.Feil@hotmail.com', '2017-04-
15 12:10:13', 0),
('amely_18', 'loseweightin18', 'Amely.Bauch91@yahoo.com',
'2018-02-06 16:48:43', 0),
('bbahringer', 'iambeau17', 'Beaulah_Bahringer@yahoo.com',
'2017-12-28 05:36:50', 0),
('little31', 'whocares31', 'Anthony_Little31@gmail.com',
'2017-06-01 21:12:11', 10),
('macejkovic73', 'jadajeda12',
'Jada.Macejkovic73@gmail.com', '2017-05-30 17:30:22', 0),
('marvin1', 'if0909mar', 'Marvin_Schulist@gmail.com',
'2017-09-09 02:30:49', 10),
('nitzsche77', 'bret77@#', 'Bret_Nitzsche77@gmail.com',
'2018-01-09 17:36:49', 0),
('noah51', '18Oct1976#51', 'Noah51@gmail.com', '2017-12-16
22:59:46', 0),
('oreillys', 'reallycool#1', 'Martine_OReilly@yahoo.com',
'2017-10-12 05:39:20', 0),
('wyattgreat', 'wyatt111', 'Wyatt_Wisozk2@gmail.com',
'2017-07-18 16:28:35', 0);

INSERT INTO rooms (id, room_type, price) VALUES
('AR', 'Archery Range', 120),
('B1', 'Badminton Court', 8),
('B2', 'Badminton Court', 8),
('MPF1', 'Multi Purpose Field', 50),
('MPF2', 'Multi Purpose Field', 60),
('T1', 'Tennis Court', 10),
('T2', 'Tennis Court', 10);
```

```
INSERT INTO bookings (id, room_id, booked_date,
booked_time, member_id, datetime_of_booking,
payment_status) VALUES
(1, 'AR', '2017-12-26', '13:00:00', 'oreillys', '2017-12-20
20:31:27', 'Paid'),
(2, 'MPF1', '2017-12-30', '17:00:00', 'noah51', '2017-12-22
05:22:10', 'Paid'),
(3, 'T2', '2017-12-31', '16:00:00', 'macejkovic73', '2017-
12-28 18:14:23', 'Paid'),
(4, 'T1', '2018-03-05', '08:00:00', 'little31', '2018-02-22
20:19:17', 'Unpaid'),
(5, 'MPF2', '2018-03-02', '11:00:00', 'marvin1', '2018-03-
01 16:13:45', 'Paid'),
(6, 'B1', '2018-03-28', '16:00:00', 'marvin1', '2018-03-23
22:46:36', 'Paid'),
(7, 'B1', '2018-04-15', '14:00:00', 'macejkovic73', '2018-
04-12 22:23:20', 'Cancelled'),
(8, 'T2', '2018-04-23', '13:00:00', 'macejkovic73', '2018-
04-19 10:49:00', 'Cancelled'),
(9, 'T1', '2018-05-25', '10:00:00', 'marvin1', '2018-05-21
11:20:46', 'Unpaid'),
(10, 'B2', '2018-06-12', '15:00:00', 'bbahringer', '2018-
05-30 14:40:23', 'Paid');

-- ************* CREATE VIEW *************

CREATE VIEW member_bookings AS
SELECT bookings.id, room_id, room_type, booked_date,
booked_time, member_id, datetime_of_booking, price,
payment_status
FROM
bookings JOIN rooms
ON
bookings.room_id = rooms.id
ORDER BY
bookings.id;

-- ************* CREATE PROCEDURES *************

DELIMITER $$

CREATE PROCEDURE insert_new_member (IN p_id VARCHAR(255),
IN p_password VARCHAR(255), IN p_email VARCHAR(255))
```

```
BEGIN
    INSERT INTO members (id, password, email) VALUES (p_id,
p_password, p_email);
END $$

CREATE PROCEDURE delete_member (IN p_id VARCHAR(255))
BEGIN
    DELETE FROM members WHERE id = p_id;
END $$

CREATE PROCEDURE update_member_password (IN p_id
VARCHAR(255), IN p_password VARCHAR(255))
BEGIN
    UPDATE members SET password = p_password WHERE id = p_id;
END $$

CREATE PROCEDURE update_member_email (IN p_id VARCHAR(255),
IN p_email VARCHAR(255))
BEGIN
    UPDATE members SET email = p_email WHERE id = p_id;
END $$

CREATE PROCEDURE make_booking (IN p_room_id VARCHAR(255),
IN p_booked_date DATE, IN p_booked_time TIME, IN
p_member_id VARCHAR(255))
BEGIN
    DECLARE v_price DECIMAL(6, 2);
    DECLARE v_payment_due DECIMAL(6, 2);
    SELECT price INTO v_price FROM rooms WHERE id =
p_room_id;
    INSERT INTO bookings (room_id, booked_date, booked_time,
member_id) VALUES (p_room_id, p_booked_date, p_booked_time,
p_member_id);
    SELECT payment_due INTO v_payment_due FROM members WHERE
id = p_member_id;
    UPDATE members SET payment_due = v_payment_due + v_price
WHERE id = p_member_id;
END $$

CREATE PROCEDURE update_payment (IN p_id INT)
BEGIN
    DECLARE v_member_id VARCHAR(255);
    DECLARE v_payment_due DECIMAL(6, 2);
```

```
    DECLARE v_price DECIMAL(6, 2);
    UPDATE bookings SET payment_status = 'Paid' WHERE id =
p_id;
    SELECT member_id, price INTO v_member_id, v_price FROM
member_bookings WHERE id = p_id;
    SELECT payment_due INTO v_payment_due FROM members WHERE
id = v_member_id;
    UPDATE members SET payment_due = v_payment_due - v_price
WHERE id = v_member_id;
END $$


CREATE PROCEDURE view_bookings (IN p_id VARCHAR(255))
BEGIN
    SELECT * FROM member_bookings WHERE id = p_id;
END $$


CREATE PROCEDURE search_room (IN p_room_type VARCHAR(255),
IN p_booked_date DATE, IN p_booked_time TIME)
BEGIN
    SELECT * FROM rooms WHERE id NOT IN (SELECT room_id FROM
bookings WHERE booked_date = p_booked_date AND booked_time
= p_booked_time AND payment_status != 'Cancelled') AND
room_type = p_room_type;
END $$


CREATE PROCEDURE cancel_booking (IN p_booking_id INT, OUT
p_message VARCHAR(255))
BEGIN
    DECLARE v_cancellation INT;
    DECLARE v_member_id VARCHAR(255);
    DECLARE v_payment_status VARCHAR(255);
    DECLARE v_booked_date DATE;
    DECLARE v_price DECIMAL(6, 2);
    DECLARE v_payment_due VARCHAR(255);
    SET v_cancellation = 0;
    SELECT member_id, booked_date, price, payment_status INTO
v_member_id, v_booked_date, v_price, v_payment_status FROM
member_bookings WHERE id = p_booking_id;
    SELECT payment_due INTO v_payment_due FROM members WHERE
id = v_member_id;
    IF curdate() >= v_booked_date THEN
        SELECT 'Cancellation cannot be done on/after the
booked date' INTO p_message;
```

```sql
        ELSEIF v_payment_status = 'Cancelled' OR
v_payment_status = 'Paid' THEN
        SELECT 'Booking has already been cancelled or paid'
INTO p_message;
    ELSE
        UPDATE bookings SET payment_status = 'Cancelled'
WHERE id = p_booking_id;
        SET v_payment_due = v_payment_due - v_price;
        SET v_cancellation = check_cancellation
(p_booking_id);
        IF v_cancellation >= 2 THEN SET v_payment_due =
v_payment_due + 10;
        END IF;
        UPDATE members SET payment_due = v_payment_due WHERE
id = v_member_id;
        SELECT 'Booking Cancelled' INTO p_message;
    END IF;
END $$


-- ************* CREATE TRIGGER *************

CREATE TRIGGER payment_check BEFORE DELETE ON members FOR
EACH ROW
BEGIN
    DECLARE v_payment_due DECIMAL(6, 2);
    SELECT payment_due INTO v_payment_due FROM members WHERE
id = OLD.id;
    IF v_payment_due > 0 THEN
        INSERT INTO pending_terminations (id, email,
payment_due) VALUES (OLD.id, OLD.email, OLD.payment_due);
    END IF;
END $$


-- ************* CREATE FUNCTION *************

CREATE FUNCTION check_cancellation (p_booking_id INT)
RETURNS INT DETERMINISTIC
BEGIN
    DECLARE v_done INT;
    DECLARE v_cancellation INT;
    DECLARE v_current_payment_status VARCHAR(255);
    DECLARE cur CURSOR FOR
```

```sql
    SELECT payment_status FROM bookings WHERE member_id =
(SELECT member_id FROM bookings WHERE id = p_booking_id)
ORDER BY datetime_of_booking DESC;
    DECLARE CONTINUE HANDLER FOR NOT FOUND SET v_done = 1;
    SET v_done = 0;
    SET v_cancellation = 0;
    OPEN cur;
    cancellation_loop : LOOP
        FETCH cur INTO v_current_payment_status;
        IF v_current_payment_status != 'Cancelled' OR v_done =
1 THEN LEAVE cancellation_loop;
        ELSE SET v_cancellation =  v_cancellation + 1;
        END IF;
    END LOOP;
    CLOSE cur;
    RETURN v_cancellation;
END $$
DELIMITER ;
```

test.sql

```sql
SELECT * FROM members;
SELECT * FROM pending_terminations;
SELECT * FROM bookings;
SELECT * FROM rooms;

CALL insert_new_member ('angelolott', '1234abcd',
'AngeloNLott@gmail.com');

SELECT * FROM members ORDER BY member_since DESC;

CALL delete_member ('afeil');
CALL delete_member ('little31');
SELECT * FROM members;
SELECT * FROM pending_terminations;

CALL update_member_password ('noah51', '18Oct1976');
CALL update_member_email ('noah51', 'noah51@hotmail.com');
SELECT * FROM members;

SELECT * FROM members WHERE id = 'marvin1';
SELECT * FROM bookings WHERE member_id = 'marvin1';
```

```
CALL update_payment (9);
SELECT * FROM members WHERE id = 'marvin1';
SELECT * FROM bookings WHERE member_id = 'marvin1';

CALL search_room('Archery Range', '2017-12-26',
'13:00:00');

CALL search_room('Badminton Court', '2018-04-15',
'14:00:00');

CALL search_room('Badminton Court', '2018-06-12',
'15:00:00');

CALL make_booking ('AR', '2017-12-26', '13:00:00',
'noah51');

CALL make_booking ('T1', CURDATE() + INTERVAL 2 WEEK,
'11:00:00',  'noah51');
CALL make_booking ('AR', CURDATE() + INTERVAL 2 WEEK,
'11:00:00',  'macejkovic73');
SELECT * FROM bookings;
SELECT * FROM members;

CALL cancel_booking(1, @message);
SELECT @message;

CALL cancel_booking(12, @message);
SELECT @message;

CALL cancel_booking(13, @message);
SELECT @message;

SELECT * FROM members;
```

Index

Made in the USA
Monee, IL
08 August 2023